Recipes shared in
celebration of family. . .

# FAMILY
# CREATIONS

Artist
Lynn Knight Johnson

Publisher
Volunteer Auxiliaries of
The Gladney Fund

The 22 Volunteer Auxiliaries of The Gladney Fund, located throughout the Southwest and Northeast United States and the Carolinas, support members involved in the adoption process, promote adoption through public education, and raise funds for The Gladney Center.

Proceeds from the sale of FAMILY CREATIONS will go to The Gladney Fund to support services and programs at The Gladney Center that benefit the adoption triad: birth mothers, adoptive parents, and their children. They include pre and post adoption counseling, prenatal maternity care, infant delivery, adoption outreach education, adoption records maintenance, and capital improvements on Gladney's campus.

Additional copies of FAMILY CREATIONS may be obtained at the cost of $15.95, plus $3.00 postage and handling charge, for each book. Use order forms in back of book and make checks payable to The Gladney Fund. Send to:

FAMILY CREATIONS
Madison Square Station
P.O. Box 1152
New York, N.Y. 10159

ISBN 0-9642357-0-6

First printing: 5,000 copies, November 1994

Printed in the USA by

**WIMMER**
The Wimmer Companies, Inc.
Memphis • Dallas

# DEDICATION

FAMILY CREATIONS is dedicated to
The Gladney Center
which has created thousands of families through adoption,
changing our lives forever...and the way we cook!
and
The families and friends of Gladney
who shared their prized recipes, spent long hours testing and tasting,
and unselfishly gave of their time and creative ideas.

With special thanks to
The original Cookbook Committee (now busy with babies);
Lynn Johnson for giving life to this book;
Sarah Fleming, Marlene Kalajian, Dawn Margolis, and Janet Presley;
Ed Crane, Ellen Wilson, and Judy Hayes
for invaluable guidance and support; and

The Auxiliary Chairmen who helped make this book possible:

| | |
|---|---|
| Mandy Ashlock | Jackie Meyer |
| Susan Atchison | Kim Miers |
| Kathy Buroker | Darcey Moran |
| Pam Dawson | Dawn Oddo |
| Libby Grafa | Maryann Testa |
| Louise Havlicek | Cindy Walker |
| Ginger Hebert | Nancy Walters |
| Barbara Hill | Vicki Wilcox |
| Nanou Knisely | Shari Lynn Wilfong |
| Cynthia Larkin | Nan Williams |

Our hearts to Jim for spending early morning hours with Tyler;
Grampa for his keen eye;
Brian for sharing his space and computer know-how;
and Alex Callan, at last!

The Cookbook "Committee"
Tacey Carroll
Sherri Schexnayder

# CONTRIBUTORS

## Abilene
Dana Caldwell
Judy Kreitman
Donna Martin
Jamie Mathis
Melody McGuire
Kim Miers
Jodie Minze
Lee Ann Robinson
Betina Williams

## Acadiana
Phyllis Berberich
Shawn Hebert
Barbara Hebert
Debbie Lokey
Debra Meaux
Carol Mestayer
Nina Ravey
Sandra Ransonet
Kathy Rosenberg

## Arkansas
Kathleen Beattie
Lou Beighley
Beth Carty
Nancy Clowers
Nancy Downing
Debbie Hashem
Jill Hickerson
Kay Jaco
Penne Jacobs
Lynn Jenkins
Paula Kalina
Edna Koehler
Gail Moore
Tricia Rhodes
Patricia Smith
Joyce Smith
Jafa Smith
René Starr
Frances Waldron
Cindy Walker
Beverly Watkins

## Austin
Christine Anderson
Brenda Berger
Gayle Clark
Freda Hamric
Leslie Hans
Rose Hutyra
Nanou Knisely
Sara Mackie
Bob and Mary
    Scarborough
Marion Smith
Sobel Catering
Marcia Sobel-Fox
Peggy Sterling
Amy Younkman

## Capital Area
Carolyn Gorley
Louise Havlicek
Susan MacDonald
Margaret Schaeffer
Sally Simmons

## Central Oklahoma
Cynthia Archiniaco
Rebecca Brawley
Peggy Duncan
Shawn Grizzle
Linda Harris
Mary Henneke
Barbara Hill
Susan Jernigan
Anita Jones
Linda Kongs
Susan Robertson
Deanna Ryser
Beth Shortt
Susan Stussi
Leanne Galloway
    Waddell
Marsha Ward

## Central Texas
Tommy Goodrich

Kay Goodrich
Sherry Kroll
Joan Palesota
Debbie Quebe
Debbie Sulak
Shari Lynn Wilfong

## Dallas
Paula Burford
Margaret Caverlee
Janet Daulton
Barbara Farmer
Meg Henderson
Camille Kress
Cynthia Larkin
Linda Lockwood
Nancy McAllister
Carolyn Perry
Michelle Ann Rickoff
Cheryl Salanty
Karen Singler
Sarah St. Laurent
Anne Tierney
Mary Wade
Cindy Ward
Marilyn Weber

## East Texas
Kathy Buroker
Rhonda Barnes
Sherry Charter
Janet Harrison
Joyce Milburn

## Lubbock
Mandy Ashlock
Gina Gilbert
Billie Hibbitt
Jessica Lynch
Trena Thomasson

## North Carolina
Ann Hatchett
Nancy Williams

## New Orleans

Cynthia Babst
Susan Bourgeois
Linda Christovich
Cindy Denson
Ann Gauthier
Victoria Hereford
Karen Hickey
Dawn Oddo
Linda Scioneaux
Toots Villere
Linda Vincent
Bonnie Waters

## New York

Joanne Agoglia
Debbie Bass
Marijane Bates
Betsy Boyle
Mary Bushnell
Tacey Carroll
Tracy Caudle
Hope Challak
Becky Decker
Susan Diehl
Sarah Fleming
Lynn Halbfinger
Kathleen Hall
Joan Henle
Shannon Hennessey
Sharon Hersch
Linda Jones
Marleen Kalajian
Barbara Kelly
Adrienne Kirby
Ann Kriete
Helen Krumm
Rosemary Lamie
Natalie Lardner
Nancy Lisnow
Carole Littlefield
Cathie Littlefield
Jeanne Mackin
Dawn Margolis
Charlotte McGee
Anna McGinn
Sharon Meadows
Judith Moore
Gail Paonessa

Nora Peyton
Martha Phillips
Tyler Phillips
Nancy Restuccia
Michele Sandlass
Joyce Scallan
Sherri Schexnayder
Kelly Smith
Karen Talbot
Stevie Thompson
Ellen Wales
Kendra Wales
Frances Weindling
Rosanne Young
Anabel Zabolio

## Permian Basin

Susan Atchison
Nancy Cooper
Joni Fields
Barbara Reed

## San Angelo

Jane Landers

## San Antonio

Kelly Lancaster
Nikki Dan
Jerry McDavid
Cyndee Dubinski
Karen Munroe
Margaret Mitchell

## Southeast Pennsylvania

Jeanne Annarelli
Craig Bigger
Patricia Bigger
Jean Brennan
Hope Chollak
Mary Ehret
Barbara Felzer
Laura Fishbein
Barbara Fitts
Linda Grimes
Pam Hammock
Marie Lazar
Susan McCarter
Marla Moskovitz

Lisa Rotfeld
Susan Smith
Carol Stern
Nancy Walters

## Southeast Texas

Karen Agnew
Susan Burke
Brenda Farris
Zachery Farris
Stephanie Farris
Elizabeth Jolly
JayLynn Lavergne
Adele Reeder
Charlotte Reeder
Dianne Smith
Katheryn White
Marie Williams

## Tarrant County

Kathleen Frye Atkinson
Lee Ann Blum
Jeanne Breaux
Marilyn Broussard
Susan Bryson
Dee Ann Crawford
Tracey Ezelle
Kathleen Frye
Beckie Geren
Kathe Goodwin
Sandy Gress
John and Amy Hawrylak
Ruth Ann Meek
Charlotte Melster
Jana Moore
Net Musfeldt
Charlotte Meester
Nancy Parker
Betty Rutherford
Laura Seidel
Debbie Sewell
Brenda Swayze
Teri Thatcher
Cindy Wells
Mary Helen Wells
Martha Williams

## Texas Panhandle

Pam Dawson

## Tulsa

Suzanne Albright
Kelley Bently
Susan Billingsly
Rene Bohmer
Teresa Caruso
Maggie Harris
Nancy Hicks
Casie Lewis
Rhonda Liggett
Darcey Moran
Peggy Murray
Irene Osgood
Jeanne Osgood

Linda Pogue
Ann Radford
Jody Radford
Elaine Reneau
Margo Reneau
Dianne Renkes
Jean Ronketty
Ada Scott
Darrell Scott
Lovena Scott
Vickie Smith
Jamie Taylor
Patricia Washington
Joan Willoughby
Mary Woods

## Gladney

Diana Bradford
Celeste Cantrell
Heidi Cox
Ed Crane
Shane Ferrell
Judy Hayes
Pattye Hicks
Cathy Salamone Leach
Lezlee Martin
Kelly Nelson
Kim Pacheco
Melanie Skillman
Debbie Thomson
Zemly Turner

*We thank each of you for your contribution and sincerely hope that no name has been omitted or mispelled.*

# About Gladney

*Adoption is a lifelong process,*
*and those who choose to work with Gladney*
*become part of 'The Gladney Family.'*

The Gladney Center has been creating families since 1887. Founded by The Reverend I.Z.T. Morris and fueled by the vision of Edna Gladney, The Gladney Center has allowed young women to reshape their lives, while giving more than 23,000 children and more than 10,000 couples the precious gift of family.

The Gladney Center provides ongoing, high quality services to all members of the adoption triad: birth mothers, adoptive parents, and their children.

## Birth Mothers

A young woman who plans adoption through The Gladney Center (over 400 annually) may choose to live on Gladney's Fort Worth, Texas, headquarters campus or participate in its Community Services program while living at home. In either case, she will work with caring, dedicated counselors and receive private medical care, comprehensive educational opportunities, and career guidance.

## Adoptive Parents

Those interested in creating their families through adoption have access to several programs in addition to Gladney's traditional agency-assisted adoption. They include international adoption, minority adoption, and designated adoption.

## The Children

*The ultimate goal of Gladney's adoption program*
*has been and always will be*
*to provide the best homes for children entrusted to its care.*

With openness and flexibility in the adoption process, Gladney works with birth mothers and adoptive parents to create an adoption plan that is best for all of them and, most importantly, for the child.

Adoptees, as well as birth mothers and adoptive parents, have lifelong access to Gladney's Post Adoption Department. Its unique services include maintenance of all adoption records; sharing of information, if desired; and adoption counseling and education.

## GLADNEY'S VOLUNTEER AUXILIARIES

Gladney commits more time and resources to educate the public about adoption than any other private or government organization, and volunteers play a major role in Gladney's outreach efforts.

Over 1,800 families belong to one of Gladney's 22 volunteer auxiliary support groups located throughout the Southwest and Northeast U.S. and in the Carolinas.

In addition to raising funds for Gladney and promoting adoption, each auxiliary provides support for members waiting to adopt and those parenting and opportunities for their children to grow up with other adopted children.

Over the past two years, the auxiliaries have worked together to create this cookbook as an ongoing funding source and outreach tool for Gladney.

Those of us who know the joy of having a baby placed in our arms want to ensure that The Gladney Center remains strong and secure in the future—ready to help families yet to be created.

Thank you for being part of our Gladney Family and its future.

# TABLE OF CONTENTS

# INTRODUCTION

FAMILY CREATIONS is a collection of over 350 recipes that reflect the exciting flavors and geographic diversity of Gladney's 22 auxiliaries, from Tex-Mex to Louisiana Cajun to New York Italian.

The recipes have been carefully tested and selected with an emphasis on fresh and surprising ingredients and ease of preparation. The aim is to inspire the whole family to cook and to make ordinary family meals extraordinary. The results: delicious family creations!

A few recipes are time consuming and worth every minute; be prepared for standing ovations! Some recipes are low fat, low cholesterol; others are definitely not.

Our advice: indulge your family in moderation. Using this book's great variety of recipes and a health-conscious balancing act, you can combine rich dishes with those that will make your total meal nutritious.

Let Creative Menus help you greet that once dreaded question: "What's for dinner?" with a twinkle in your eye. Explore kitchen secrets from families across the country. Discover pasta and vegetarian dishes that will pleasantly surprise even your pickiest eater. Next rainy Sunday, turn to Kids' Creations and turn your kids on to the fun of cooking.

We share our Gladney recipes in celebration of family—however created—and hope these recipes become a special part of your family for generations to come.

Creative

MENUS

# Healthy Creations

### Vegetarian Italian Style

Tuscan Olive Spread, 21

Caesar Salad, 81
Spinach Lasagna, 145

Fruit Pizza, 210

### Vegetarian Mexican Style

Guacamole:
The Real Thing, 24

Vegetarian Chili, 150
Mexican Cornbread, 57

Apricot Parfait, 211

### Flu Season

Hot Buttered Rum Punch, 41
(For Mom & Dad)

Aunt B.B.'s Shrimp Gumbo, 73
Granny Roux's Dilly Bread, 56

Apple Crisp, 210

### Post Holiday Blues

Snappy Tortilla Soup, 74
Patsy's Cornbread, 57

Winter Fruit with Lemon
Yogurt Sauce, 211

### Pool's Opening — Eke!!

Dolly's Dip with
Raw Vegetables, 23

Marinated Swordfish
with Salsa, 134
Orzo & Pine Nut Pilaf, 170

### Mama Mia!!

Spinach Salad, 80

Penne with Broccoflower, 142
White Garlic Pizza, 153

Heavenly Shortcake, 184

# MIDWEEK DINNERS WITH FLAIR

## THANKSGIVING IN JULY

Grilled Honey Mustard
Chicken, 115
Roasted Vegetables, 160
Sweet Potato Casserole, 165

Cranberry Mold, 77

No-Guilt Pumpkin Pie, 205

## CAJUN NIGHT

Spedini, 21
Cajun Broccoli-Cauliflower
Soup, 67

New Orleans Red Beans
& Rice, 113
Creole Eggplant, 158

Creole Cake, 186

## SOMEWHERE OVER THE RAINBOW

Greek Bread, 22

Texas Indonesian Pork, 110
Karen's Rice Pilaf, 169
Herbed Broccoli, 157

Caribbean Fudge Pie, 205

## THERE'S NO PLACE LIKE HOME

Moore Meat Loaf, Please, 99
Spaghetti Squash, 161
French Fries without Frying, 164

Mother's Apple Cobbler, 209

## BACK IN YOUR OWN BACKYARD

Hidden Treasure Salad, 78
Aunt Nita's Marinated
Flank Steak, 104
Jalapeño Corn & Rice
Casserole, 166

Grizzle's Spice Cake, 187

# MOSTLY FOR DADS & KIDS

## MOM'S MORNING TO SLEEP IN

Almond Tea, 41

Applesauce Muffins, 45
Day Before French Toast, 64
Breakfast Sausage Ring, 62

## DADDY & KIDS DO DINNER

Meatball Soup, 75
Cheese Garlic Biscuits, 58

Aunt Mary's Faux Éclairs, 239

## REPORT CARD DAY

Cheese Crispies, 19

Oven-Fried Sesame Chicken, 120
Hot Potato Salad, 83

Banana Smoothies, 224
Report Card Day Cookies, 232

## RAINY DAY FUN

Porcupine Salad, 228

Porcupine Meatballs, 228
Granny's White Bread, 225

Flower Pot Dessert, 234

## DAD'S TEX-MEX SURPRISE PARTY

Gazpacho, 73

Southwest Beef Enchiladas, 95
Chicken Enchiladas
Florentine, 127
Midland Dirty Rice, 167
Southwestern Black Bean
Salad, 85

Mexican Sheet Cake, 188

# ENTERTAINING FAMILY & FRIENDS

## MOM & DAD MEET MR. RIGHT

Southwestern Crab Quesadilla
with Tomatillo Relish, 30

Marinated Filet Mignon, 105
Margaret's Squash Casserole, 159
Stuffed Herbed Potatoes, 163

Jersey Tomatoes with
Herb Dressing, 79

Chocolate Paradise Pie, 206

## NEW YEAR'S BRUNCH IN SEPTEMBER

Champagne Punch, 41
Salmon Mousse, 34

Britt's Favorite Beef Brisket, 103
Challah French Toast, 63
Apricot-Pineapple Kugel, 53
Mango Mold, 78

Schnechen, 52

## GIGI & PAPA'S FALL VISIT

Louise's Pumpkin Soup, 69

Cornish Hens with Pecan
Stuffing, 128
Glazed Carrots & Onions, 158
Kay's Potato Casserole, 161

Brown Bag Apple Pie, 202

## THREE-FAMILY BARBECUE

Highway Department Punch, 42
Southwest Cheesecake, 29

Pasta Harvest Salad, 87
Bamboo-Skewered Chicken, 115
Honey-Mustard Pork
Tenderloin, 110
Sweet & Sour Potato Salad, 83
Gram's Cole Slaw, 82

Grandma Todey's Brownies, 177
Raisin Bars, 179

## NEW MOM LUNCHEON

Easy Spiced Tea, 42

Spiced Plum Soup, 68

Martha's Cheese Bread, 49
Mom's Pumpkin Bread, 48

Mrs. Bolton's Broccoli Salad, 80
Deanna's Chicken Salad, 92

English Trifle, 214

# CREATIVE WAYS TO LOSE THE FAT AND FIND THE FLAVOR

**Use non-stick oil sprays and non-stick cookware.**
They allow cooking with little or no fat.

**Use non-fat chicken broth.**
Sauté with 1 teaspoon olive oil (per serving), adding non-fat chicken broth, plain water, and/or white wine as needed.

**Steam or microwave vegetables.**

**Undress salads.**
Sprinkle a variety of fresh greens with 1 tablespoon (per serving) grated Parmesan or crumbled feta cheese and lots of fresh pepper. If dressing, try equal parts olive oil and balsamic vinegar.

**Cook with fresh herbs and add flavor with condiments.**
To find flavor lost when fat is removed, cook with herbs and add fancy mustards and horseradish; savory vegetables like onion, garlic, and peppers; orange and lemon juice or zest. Try garlic-dill marinade for shellfish: equal parts olive oil and fresh lemon juice, chopped fresh dill, and garlic.

**Marinate, marinate, marinate! Then broil or grill.**
Mexican salsas, fat-free pasta and teriyaki sauces make great marinades. Try zesty yogurt for chicken and lamb: ¾ cup yogurt, 4 tablespoons lemon juice, minced onion and garlic, ½ teaspoon each cumin and curry, ¼ teaspoon each cinnamon and cloves, salt, and pepper.

**Remove skin from chicken.**
Dip skinless chicken into egg white or skim milk then coat with seasoned bread or corn flake crumbs to keep moist during baking.

**Cut oil and sugar in baked goods.**
Add applesauce, mashed bananas, and/or dried fruit. Use fewer nuts, coarsely chopped. For 1 whole egg, use 2 egg whites.

**Substitute lower fat dairy products.**
For cream, evaporated skim milk. For whipped cream, whip ⅓ cup heavy cream until stiff then fold in ⅔ cup non-fat yogurt. For sour cream, equal parts non-fat yogurt and low-fat cottage cheese.

# APPETIZERS
# & BEVERAGES

## Dips & Spreads

## Cold Appetizers

## Hot Appetizers

## Mexican

## Seafood
### Cold

### Hot

## Beverages

# CHEESE CRISPIES

2 sticks margarine, room temperature
1/2 pound extra sharp Cheddar cheese, coarsely grated
2 cups flour
1/2 teaspoon salt
1/4 teaspoon red pepper (more if desired)
2 cups Rice Crispies

1. Preheat oven to 325°.
2. Blend margarine and cheese.
3. Mix flour, salt, and red pepper. Gradually add to cheese mixture and combine with hands.
4. Add Rice Crispies to dough and shape into little balls. Press each ball with thumb and place on ungreased cookie sheet.
5. Bake at 325° for 20-30 minutes until golden brown. Store loosely covered in dry place.

**Yields 5-6 dozen.**

*Also good crumbled as topping on soup or salad.*

# ONION CHEESE PUFFS

1 loaf thinly sliced bread
1 onion, finely chopped
1 tablespoon butter
1 (8-ounce) package cream cheese, softened
1 tablespoon grated Parmesan cheese
1 tablespoon mayonnaise
1 teaspoon Dijon mustard
Dash of Worcestershire sauce
6 drops Tabasco sauce
1/4 teaspoon salt
Paprika for topping

1. Preheat oven to 350°.
2. Cut bread into 50 1" rounds with biscuit or cookie cutter.
3. Sauté onion in butter and set aside.
4. With electric mixer, combine all other ingredients and spread on bread rounds.
5. Top bread rounds with onions and sprinkle with paprika.
6. Place on cookie sheet and bake at 350° for about 10 minutes until golden brown.

**Yields 50 puffs.**

# VEGETABLE CHEESE SQUARES

2 cups finely chopped raw or parboiled vegetables such as broccoli, red or green peppers, carrots, onions, black olives, etc.
1 (8-ounce) package crescent rolls
1 (8-ounce) package cream cheese, softened
1/3 cup ranch-style dressing
1 teaspoon dill
1 cup shredded Cheddar or Monterey Jack cheese

1. Prepare colorful variety of vegetables.
2. To make crust, unroll crescent rolls and gently pat into ungreased 13" x 9" x 2" baking dish. Bake according to package directions. Cool on wire rack.
3. Combine cream cheese, dressing, and dill. Spread evenly over cooled crust.
4. Top with vegetables and shredded cheese and press gently into cream cheese mixture.
5. Chill 1 hour before serving, then cut into small squares.

**Yields 30 squares.**

# SHIRLEY'S ARTICHOKE SQUARES

2 (6-ounce) jars marinated artichoke hearts, drained and chopped with marinade reserved from 1 jar
1 small onion, finely chopped
1 garlic clove, minced
4 eggs
1/2 cup fine bread crumbs
1/4 teaspoon salt
1/8 teaspoon black pepper
1/8 teaspoon oregano
1/8 teaspoon Tabasco sauce
1/2 pound sharp Cheddar cheese, shredded
2 tablespoons chopped parsley

1. Preheat oven to 325°.
2. Sauté onion and garlic in reserved marinade until wilted. Drain and set aside.
3. Beat eggs well. Stir in bread crumbs, salt, pepper, oregano, and Tabasco.
4. Add artichokes, sautéed onion and garlic, and cheese. Mix well.
5. Turn artichoke mixture into greased 11" x 7" x 2" baking dish. Sprinkle with parsley, then bake at 325° for 30 minutes.
6. Cool slightly and cut into small squares. Serve warm.

**Yields 4 dozen small squares.**

# SPEDINI

1 20" loaf French or Italian bread
1/4 cup chopped yellow onion
1/2 stick butter
1-2 tablespoons yellow mustard
1 tablespoon poppy seeds
1/2 pound Swiss cheese, sliced
6 slices bacon

1. Preheat oven to 350°.

2. Remove top crust and make about 10 cuts into bread, each cut about halfway through (electric knife makes this easier). Place bread on cookie sheet.

3. Sauté onion in butter. Remove from heat and add mustard and poppy seeds. Spoon onion mixture into cuts of bread.

4. Fold Swiss cheese slices and insert one folded slice into each cut of bread.

5. Arrange bacon on top on bread. Bake at 350° for 15 minutes then put under broiler for about 2 minutes to crisp bacon. (Watch carefully.)

6. To serve, cut completely through bread and serve hot.

**Yields 20 pieces.**

# TUSCAN OLIVE SPREAD

1 cup Calamata olives, pitted
2 teaspoons capers
2 garlic cloves
1/4 cup extra virgin olive oil
1 tablespoon fresh Italian parsley
1 loaf French or Italian bread, cut in 1/4" slices and lightly toasted

1. Mince olives, capers, and garlic in food processor. Add olive oil and parsley until parsley is chopped and ingredients well blended.

2. Spread olive mixture on toasted bread slices.

**Yields 1 cup.**

# GREEK BREAD

1 loaf French or Italian bread
1/4 cup butter or margarine
2 cups grated mozzarella cheese
6 green onions, chopped
1 (4 1/4-ounce) can black olives, pitted and chopped
1/2 teaspoon garlic powder

1. Preheat oven to 350°.
2. Cut bread in half lengthwise and place on cookie sheet.
3. Melt butter in large bowl in microwave and add remaining ingredients.
4. Spread olive mixture on bread and bake at 350° for 20 minutes.
5. Slice cooked bread into 2" pieces and serve warm.

**Serves 8.**

*Can substitute mushrooms for olives.*

# MUSHROOM BREAD

1 (8-ounce) package refrigerated crescent rolls
2 cups sliced fresh mushrooms
3 tablespoons butter or margarine, melted
1 cup grated mozzarella cheese
1/4 cup grated Parmesan cheese
1/4 teaspoon Italian seasoning (or garlic powder)

1. Preheat oven to 375°.
2. Separate dough into triangles. Place on 13" pizza pan or baking stone. Pinch seams together to make one big square.
3. Toss sliced mushrooms in melted butter to coat. Arrange mushrooms on top of dough.
4. Sprinkle with cheeses and Italian seasoning. Bake at 375° for 20 minutes.
5. Cut into wedges or squares with pizza cutter. Serve warm.

**Serves 8-10.**

# HOLIDAY CHEESE WREATH

1 pound sharp Cheddar
cheese, grated
1 cup mayonnaise
1 cup chopped pecans
1/2 cup chopped green onions
1 tablespoon Worcestershire
sauce
1 (10-ounce) jar strawberry
jam

1. Blend first 5 ingredients and
mold on tray as a wreath.
2. Put strawberry jam in center and
place buttery crackers around
cheese ring just before serving.

**Serves 35-40.**

# TASTY COTTAGE CHEESE DIP

1 (24-ounce) container small
curd cottage cheese
1 (16-ounce) container sour
cream
1 cup shredded Cheddar
cheese
1 medium cucumber, finely
chopped
1 small red onion, minced
4-5 kosher dill pickles, finely
chopped
1 package green onion dip
mix
Black pepper to taste
Celery and garlic salt, to taste

1. Mix all ingredients well.
2. Refrigerate until chilled and
serve with vegetables or chips.

**Yields 4 cups.**

# DOLLY'S DIP

3/4 cup mayonnaise
4 1/2 teaspoons ketchup
4 1/2 teaspoons grated onion
4 1/2 teaspoons honey
1 1/2 teaspoons lemon juice
1 1/2 teaspoons curry powder

1. Mix ingredients together, adding
one at a time in order listed.
2. Chill and serve with raw vegetables.

**Yields 1 1/2 cups.**

# CLASSIC DIP

1 (8-ounce) package cream cheese, softened
1 envelope Good Seasons Zesty Italian salad dressing mix
1 (8-ounce) plain yogurt
1 tablespoon milk

1. Beat all ingredients together in small bowl until well blended.
2. Refrigerate. Serve with raw vegetables.

**Yields 2 cups.**

*Also great as topping for baked potato.*

# GUACAMOLE: THE REAL THING

4 medium, ripe avocados
1 small onion
1 garlic clove
1 cup fresh cilantro leaves, packed
1- 2 small, hot chilies, seeded
1 tablespoon lemon juice
Salt to taste
1 cup chopped tomato

1. Cut avocados in half lengthwise, remove and save one pit. Scoop out pulp into large bowl and coarsely mash with fork or potato masher.
2. In food processor, mince onion, garlic, cilantro, and chilies. Add these ingredients to avocados.
3. Stir in lemon juice and salt to taste. Add tomatoes.
4. Place pit back in the guacamole to prevent browning and refrigerate for at least 15 minutes and preferably not more than 1 hour.
5. Remove pit before serving and serve with tortilla chips and/or raw vegetables.

**Yields 3 cups.**

# "SPIKED" GUACAMOLE

2 large avocados
4 heaping tablespoons plain
  yogurt
2 teaspoons mayonnaise
4 drops Tabasco sauce
½ teaspoon soy sauce
¼ teaspoon coarse black
  pepper
¼ teaspoon ginger
⅛ teaspoon cayenne pepper
1 garlic clove, minced
1 teaspoon Spike seasoning

1. Combine all ingredients in bowl.
2. Refrigerate with avocado pit to prevent browning. Remove pit and serve with tortilla chips.

**Yields 2 cups.**

# ARKANSAS GUACAMOLE

3 large avocados, mashed
1 small onion, grated
1-2 (4-ounce) cans chopped
  green chilies
1 tablespoon garlic juice
2-3 tablespoons lemon juice
3 tablespoons mayonnaise
Salt to taste
1 cup chopped tomatoes
1 cup diced black olives

1. Mix first 7 ingredients and chill.
2. Top with tomatoes and black olives.

**Yields 2-3 cups.**

# MEXICAN PIE

¼ pound sharp Cheddar cheese, grated
¼ pound Monterey Jack cheese, grated
1 (4-ounce) can chopped green chilies
3 eggs, beaten

1. Preheat oven to 350° and grease pie plate.
2. Layer cheese then peppers then cheese in pie plate. Pour eggs over layers.
3. Cook at 350° for 30 minutes.

**Serves 6-8 as appetizer or 4 with salad for lunch.**

*Low-fat cheese and egg substitute can be used.*

# WALKING TACO

1 (16-ounce) can refried beans
½ envelope taco seasoning mix
¼ cup mayonnaise
¼ cup sour cream
1 bunch green onions, minced
2 medium tomatoes, chopped
1 large ripe avocado, chopped
1 (4½-ounce) can pitted black olives, chopped
½ cup Cheddar cheese
½ cup Monterey Jack cheese
Tortilla chips

1. Spread refried beans in bottom of platter.
2. Mix taco seasoning with mayonnaise and sour cream. Spread over beans.
3. Layer with next 6 ingredients in order given.
4. Serve with tortilla chips, dip into layers, and enjoy!

**Serves 12.**

# JALAPEÑO FUDGE

1 pound Cheddar cheese, grated
1 pound Monterey Jack cheese, grated
¾ cup chopped jalapeño peppers
2 eggs
½ cup flour
1 (5-ounce) can evaporated milk

1. Preheat oven to 350°.
2. Put half of each cheese in bottom of 13" x 9" x 2" greased pan. Cover cheeses with jalapeño peppers and top with remaining cheese.
3. Mix eggs, flour, and milk, and pour over cheeses.
4. Bake at 350° for 30 minutes. Serve warm.

**Serves 12-14.**

# MEXICAN HAT DANCE

1 (8-ounce) package cream cheese
Pinch of salt
1 (8-ounce) container sour cream
1 (9-ounce) can bean dip
½ envelope taco seasoning mix
½ cup chopped green onions
10 drops Tabasco sauce
1 cup grated Cheddar cheese
1 cup grated Monterey Jack cheese

1. Preheat oven to 350°.
2. Mix all ingredients with half the cheeses.
3. Place mixture in 13" x 9" x 2" casserole dish and sprinkle with remaining cheeses.
4. Cover with foil and bake at 350° for 20 minutes. Serve with tortilla chips.

**Serves 12-14.**

# MEXICAN-CAJUN DELIGHT

## BOTTOM LAYER

2 (¼-ounce) envelopes
  unflavored gelatin
½ cup hot water
2 large avocados, chopped
2 large avocados, pureed
½ cup finely chopped onion
3 tablespoons lemon juice
4 tablespoons mayonnaise
½ teaspoon salt
½ teaspoon black pepper
¼ teaspoon red pepper sauce

## MIDDLE LAYER

¼ cup finely chopped green
  onions
½ cup finely chopped celery
½ cup finely chopped bell
  pepper
1 pound fresh mushrooms,
  sliced
2 tablespoons butter
1 pound crabmeat
1 pound boiled shrimp, finely
  chopped
1 (8-ounce) package cream
  cheese
½ teaspoon salt
½ teaspoon black pepper
½ teaspoon powdered steak
  seasoning
½ teaspoon garlic powder
¼ teaspoon red pepper
¼ cup dissolved gelatin

## TOP LAYER

1 cup sour cream
2 tablespoons finely chopped
  onion
1 avocado, sliced for garnish

1. For bottom layer, dissolve gelatin in water and set aside. In another bowl, combine remaining ingredients. Stir in ¼ cup dissolved gelatin. Spoon into springform pan, cover, and refrigerate for about 30 minutes.

2. For middle layer, sauté green onions, celery, bell pepper, and mushrooms in butter until transparent. Add remaining ingredients, adjust seasonings, and cool. Spread over bottom layer and chill for about 15 minutes.

3. For top layer, combine sour cream and onion and spread over middle layer. Cover and refrigerate 8 hours until set.

4. Remove sides of pan. Garnish with sliced avocado. Serve with tortilla chips.

**Serves 20.**

*Will keep approximately 2 days, refrigerated.*

*Hard but worth it!*

# SOUTHWEST CHEESECAKE

2 (8-ounce) packages cream cheese, softened
2 cups shredded Cheddar cheese
2 cups sour cream, divided
1 envelope taco seasoning
3 eggs, room temperature
1 (4-ounce) can chopped green chilies
2/3 cup salsa

1. Preheat oven to 350°.
2. Combine cheeses and beat until fluffy. Stir in 1 cup sour cream and taco seasoning. Beat in eggs one at a time. Fold in chilies.
3. Pour into 9½" x 2½" springform pan. Bake at 350° for 35-40 minutes until center is firm. Remove from oven; cool 10 minutes.
4. Spoon remaining sour cream over top, then return to oven for 5 minutes.
5. Cool completely on wire rack and refrigerate covered overnight.
6. Remove from pan and place on serving plate. Top with salsa and serve with tortilla chips.

**Serves 25-30.**

*Big winner!*

# CRABMEAT SPREAD

1 (6½-ounce) can crabmeat, drained and flaked
2 tablespoons chopped parsley
1 teaspoon chopped green onions
4 tablespoons mayonnaise
½ teaspoon lemon juice
1 tablespoon chili sauce
½ tablespoon horseradish

1. Combine and refrigerate.
2. Serve with crackers.

**Serves 4.**

# SOUTHWESTERN CRAB QUESADILLAS

4 tablespoons oil, divided
1 garlic clove, minced
1 small onion, chopped
1 chili pepper (poblano),
    roasted, peeled, and diced
1 pound lump crabmeat,
    picked over
3 ounces cream cheese
2 tablespoons mayonnaise
1 teaspoon salt
½ teaspoon pepper
2 tablespoons chopped fresh
    cilantro
16-20 flour tortillas
¼ cup melted butter

1. Heat 2 tablespoons oil and sauté garlic and onion for 3-5 minutes. Remove from heat and stir in next 7 ingredients. Mix well.

2. Spread crab mixture on 8-10 tortillas and top each with another tortilla. Combine melted butter and 2 tablespoons oil and brush over quesadillas.

3. Heat non-stick skillet over medium-high heat and sauté quesadillas until brown on both sides, about 3-4 minutes each side.

4. Cut tortillas into 6 triangles and serve with Tomatillo Relish.

**Yields 48-60 pieces.**

*Roast pepper by holding with fork over gas flame, rotating until charred all over. While hot, place pepper in zip-lock bag and freeze for 10 minutes. Charred skin should peel off easily.*

# TOMATILLO RELISH

1 tablespoon olive oil
2 shallots, minced
1 pound tomatillos, finely
    chopped
5½" pieces fresh or packaged
    mango, finely chopped
1-2 tablespoons minced fresh
    cilantro
Salt and white pepper to taste

1. Heat oil in small skillet and add shallots. Cook 2 minutes until softened.

2. In a bowl, combine shallots with remaining ingredients. Refrigerate up to 24 hours before serving.

**Yields 2-3 cups.**

# CRAB DIABLO

1 green pepper, chopped
1 tablespoon oil
2 (14-ounce) cans artichoke hearts, drained and chopped
½ cup chopped and drained pimentos
1 bunch green onions, thinly sliced
3 jalapeño peppers, seeded and minced
1 cup grated Parmesan cheese
4 teaspoons Worcestershire sauce
2 cups mayonnaise
2 tablespoons lemon juice
1 teaspoon seasoned pepper
1 pound crabmeat, picked over
⅓ cup lightly toasted, sliced almonds

1. Preheat oven to 375°.
2. Sauté green pepper in oil until soft. In large bowl, combine green pepper with next 10 ingredients.
3. Transfer to buttered baking dish or oven-proof chafing dish. Sprinkle with almonds.
4. Bake at 375° for 25-30 minutes until bubbly.
5. Serve with wheat thins or toasted pita triangles.

**Serves 10 or more.**

*Can prepare one day ahead.*

# EASY CRAB DIP

1 (8-ounce) package cream cheese
2 tablespoons chopped onion
1 (6½-ounce) can crabmeat
½ teaspoon white horseradish
¼ teaspoon salt
⅓ cup toasted almonds

1. Preheat oven to 375°.
2. Blend first 5 ingredients well and place in small greased casserole.
3. Sprinkle with toasted almonds, then bake at 375° for 15 minutes. Serve hot with crackers or chips.

**Serves 6-8.**

# KAREN'S ZESTY CLAM DIP

1 (8-ounce) package light cream cheese, softened
2 (6½-ounce) cans minced clams, 1 tablespoon juice reserved
2 tablespoons lemon juice
4 tablespoons Worcestershire sauce
4 green onions, minced
¼ cup mayonnaise
1 tablespoon Dijon mustard
2 dashes Tabasco sauce

1. Combine all ingredients. Mix well.
2. Serve with crackers, potato chips, or crudités.

**Serves 8-10.**

# SHRIMP DIP

½ cup chopped onion
½ cup chopped celery
½ cup chopped bell pepper
1 (2-ounce) jar pimentos, chopped
1 (8-ounce) package cream cheese
1 pint mayonnaise
1 teaspoon garlic powder
1 teaspoon black pepper
1 teaspoon seafood seasoning
1 teaspoon ketchup
½ teaspoon mustard
2 pounds shrimp, boiled, cleaned, and chopped

1. Mix all ingredients and chill.
2. Serve with crackers or chips.

**Yields 3 cups.**

*Even better prepared a day ahead!*

# SHRIMP TOAST

2 (4½-ounce) cans shrimp, drained and picked over
1 cup mayonnaise
1 teaspoon oregano
1 cup grated sharp Cheddar cheese
1 small onion, grated
1 loaf thinly sliced white bread, slices quartered

1. Preheat oven to 350°.
2. Mix first 5 ingredients in bowl.
3. Top each bread quarter with a tablespoon of shrimp mixture. Use as many bread squares as needed to use up shrimp mixture.
4. Place on cookie sheet and bake at 350° for 15-20 minutes. Serve hot.

**Yields about 40 squares.**

# SHRIMP PIZZA

1 (8-ounce) package cream cheese, softened
1 (12-ounce) bottle cocktail sauce
1 pound shrimp, boiled and chopped
4 ounces mozzarella cheese, grated
4 ounces Cheddar cheese, grated
8 green onions, chopped
1 small green pepper, chopped
1 small tomato, chopped
¼ cup chopped black olives
¼ cup chopped green olives
Parsley for garnish

1. Spread softened cream cheese on 12" platter. Layer remaining ingredients in order listed over cream cheese.
2. Refrigerate until served, then decorate with parsley and serve with crackers.

**Serves 12-16.**

# SALMON PÂTÉ

1 (1-pound) can salmon, drained and flaked
1 (8-ounce) package cream cheese, softened
1 tablespoon lemon juice
2 teaspoons grated onion
1 teaspoon prepared horseradish
¼ teaspoon garlic or onion salt
¼ teaspoon liquid smoke
½ cup chopped walnuts, almonds, or pecans
3 tablespoons finely chopped parsley

1. Remove any skin and bones from salmon. Combine with next 6 ingredients. Mix thoroughly, then chill several hours.

2. Combine nuts and parsley. Shape salmon mixture into 8" x 4" log. Roll in nut mixture and chill well.

3. Serve with assorted crackers.

**Serves 8-10.**

# SALMON MOUSSE

1 (¼-ounce) envelope gelatin
2 tablespoons lemon juice
2 slices onion
½ cup boiling water
½ cup mayonnaise
Paprika for color
1 teaspoon dried dill
1 (1-pound) can salmon, drained and flaked
1 cup heavy sweet cream

1. Pour gelatin into blender or food processor. Add lemon juice, onion, and water. Blend at high speed for 40 seconds.

2. Add mayonnaise, paprika, dill, and salmon. Blend briefly at high speed. Add cream in thirds, blending briefly after each addition.

3. Pour mixture into greased 3-4 cup mold and refrigerate several hours or overnight.

4. Unmold by dipping pan briefly in hot water to loosen, then turn over to remove.

5. Serve with crackers.

**Serves 8-10.**

# CHEESY CHICKEN WINGS

1 cup grated Parmesan cheese
2 tablespoons parsley
2 tablespoons oregano
2 teaspoons paprika
2 teaspoons salt
½ teaspoon black pepper
4 pounds chicken wings,
  disjointed
½ cup melted butter

1. Preheat oven to 350°.
2. For cheese mixture, mix first 6 ingredients in bowl.
3. Dip chicken wings in melted butter and then into cheese mixture, coating well.
4. Place on cookie sheet lined with foil. Bake at 350° for 1 hour until browned.

**Serves 10.**

# HERBED CHICKEN LIVER PÂTÉ

1 garlic clove, minced
1 medium onion, chopped
2 sticks butter, divided
1 pound chicken livers, rinsed
  and dried on paper towel
1 teaspoon salt
½ teaspoon pepper
1 bay leaf
⅛ teaspoon oregano
⅛ teaspoon tarragon
⅛ teaspoon thyme
2 tablespoons cognac or
  brandy
1 cup heavy cream
Parsley or other greens for
  garnish

1. Sauté garlic and onion in 1 stick butter until tender. Remove to a food processor or blender.
2. Sauté chicken livers in 1 stick butter until just pink inside. Add salt, pepper, bay leaf, oregano, tarragon, and thyme. Cover and simmer for 2 minutes. Remove bay leaf.
3. Add livers to garlic and onion. Puree. While pureeing, quickly add cognac or brandy and heavy cream.
4. Pour into a greased 4-cup mold. Chill at least 8 hours, preferably overnight.
5. Unmold onto greens and serve with toast points or crackers.

**Yields 4 cups.**

# DRUNKEN HOT DOGS

1 pound hot dogs
¾ cup bourbon
½ cup brown sugar
1½ cups ketchup
1 tablespoon chopped onion
Pinch of oregano
½ teaspoon rosemary

1.  Preheat oven to 350°.
2.  Cut hot dogs into bite-sized pieces and place in small casserole dish.
3.  Combine all other ingredients and pour over hot dogs. Bake at 350° for 1 hour.

**Serves 15.**

# JESSIE'S MEATBALLS

½ cup brown sugar
3 tablespoons soy sauce
1 tablespoon vinegar
1 tablespoon sherry
1 tablespoon cornstarch, dissolved in 1 tablespoon water
½ teaspoon ginger
½ teaspoon dry mustard
½ cup consommé
¾ cup pineapple juice
¼ cup ketchup
¾ pound lean chopped beef
Chopped water chestnuts

1.  Mix first 10 ingredients in saucepan and simmer until thickened.
2.  Shape beef into bite-sized meatballs and press water chestnut piece into each center.
3.  Brown meatballs, drain, and add to sauce. Serve warm in chafing dish.

**Serves 6.**

# CREAM CHEESE & DRIED BEEF BALL

1 (8-ounce) package cream cheese, softened
1 bunch (about 8) green onions, chopped
1 (4-ounce) jar dried beef, shredded

1.  Mix all ingredients thoroughly.
2.  Form into ball on serving tray and serve with favorite crackers.

**Serves 8.**

# EASY HAM CHEESEBALL

2 (2½-ounce) packages thinly sliced smoked ham
2 (8-ounce) packages cream cheese, softened
4 green onions, diced
3 tablespoons Worcestershire sauce

1. Dice 1 package of ham. In large mixing bowl, combine cream cheese, diced green onions, diced ham, and Worcestershire sauce. Mix thoroughly with hands.

2. Dice second package of ham and spread over cutting board. Form cream cheese mixture into ball and roll in ham, covering completely.

3. Place on a glass dish, cover with foil tent, and refrigerate overnight until served.

4. Serve with buttery crackers.

**Serves 20-25.**

# WRAPPED ASPARAGUS

24 thin asparagus spears, trimmed to 3-4"
12 slices prosciutto
2 (3-ounce) packages cream cheese with chives

1. Parboil asparagus tips for 2 minutes.

2. Trim fat from prosciutto and cut each piece lengthwise in half.

3. With knife, spread cream cheese onto each piece of prosciutto and lay 1 asparagus tip on cream cheese.

4. Wrap proscuitto around asparagus and arrange on serving tray.

**Serves 6-8.**

# MARINATED SAUSAGE

2 pounds Italian sweet
sausage

**MARINADE**
½ cup ketchup
½ cup vinegar
1 tablespoon soy sauce
½ cup brown sugar
½ teaspoon ginger

1. Cook sausage until done. Cool
   and cut into thin rounds.

2. Combine marinade ingredients.
   Marinate sausage for 24 hours.

3. Warm and serve as appetizer or
   with rice as entrée.

**Serves 6-8.**

*Kids love this!*

# SAUSAGE ROLLS (SICILIAN QUACHI)

2 (8-ounce) packages crescent
roll dough
2 pounds uncooked sausage
2 cups shredded mozzarella
cheese
2 bunches chopped green
onions
Freshly ground pepper

1. Preheat oven to 300°.

2. Unroll crescent roll dough on
   floured board or counter. Press
   seams together.

3. Layer dough with uncooked
   sausage, cheese, and green
   onions. Add fresh pepper to
   taste.

4. Roll dough like a jelly roll,
   moisten ends, seam-pinch, and
   seal. Cut into 1" slices. (Chilling
   makes slicing easier.)

5. Place on greased cookie sheet
   and sprinkle with mozzarella, if
   desired. Bake at 300° for 30
   minutes.

**Yields about 2 dozen slices.**

*Also great for breakfast or
brunch.*

# Polish Sausage on Rye

1 pound sausage
1 pound ground beef
1 pound Velveeta cheese (or Velveeta with jalapeño peppers)
1 teaspoon oregano
1 teaspoon Worcestershire sauce
2 loaves small party ryes

1. Preheat oven to 400°.
2. Brown sausage and beef. Drain fat.
3. On low heat, melt in chunks of cheese, stirring well. Add oregano and Worcestershire.
4. Spread sausage mixture on party ryes. Place on cookie sheet and bake at 400° about 10 minutes until bubbling.

**Yields about 30 party ryes.**

# Armadillo Eggs

1 (16-ounce) jar jalapeño peppers
1/4 cup grated Cheddar cheese
1 (16-ounce) package pork sausage
1 package Pillsbury Cornbread Twists

1. Preheat oven to 350°.
2. Carefully slice one side of each pepper and clean out seeds. Stuff pepper with cheese and then sausage.
3. Bake at 350° for 20-25 minutes until sausage is browned. Drain grease and let cool.
4. Wrap stuffed peppers with cornbread dough and place on foil-lined cookie sheet.
5. Bake at 350° for 10 minutes, then turn and bake 5 minutes more until browned. Serve whole or sliced with ranch-style dressing or salsa.

**Serves 6-8.**

# SUGARED NUTS

2 egg whites, stiffly beaten
1 teaspoon cinnamon
Dash of salt
1 cup sugar
3 cups pecans or walnuts
½ cup butter

1. Preheat oven to 325°.

2. Fold sugar, salt, and cinnamon into stiffly beaten egg whites. Add nuts, mixing gently to coat.

3. Melt butter in large flat pan. Spread nut mixture evenly in pan.

4. Bake at 325° for about 30 minutes, stirring every 10 minutes until deep golden brown. (Watch closely.)

5. Cool and store in tin or plastic container.

**Yields 3 cups.**

# SPICY PECANS

4 tablespoons butter
2 cups large pecan halves
4 teaspoons soy sauce
1 teaspoon seasoned salt
10 dashes Tabasco sauce

1. Preheat oven to 300°.

2. Melt butter in shallow pan. Add pecans, spreading evenly in the pan. Bake at 300° for 20 minutes, stirring occasionally.

3. In large mixing bowl, combine soy sauce, salt, and Tabasco. Add pecans, stirring to coat, then pour onto paper towels to cool.

4. Store in jars or freeze.

**Yields 2 cups.**

# CHAMPAGNE PUNCH

2 (12-ounce) cans pineapple-orange concentrate, thawed
1 (12-ounce) can lemonade concentrate, thawed
1½ quarts cranberry juice cocktail
1½ quarts water
1 quart champagne
Ice ring or raspberry sherbet (optional)

1. Chill all ingredients. In a large punch bowl, combine concentrates and cranberry juice. Stir in water and champagne.

2. Add ice ring or scoops of sherbet if desired.

**Yields 50 (½-cup) servings.**

*Decorate with ice ring of arranged citrus slices, maraschino cherries, or strawberries.*

# HOT BUTTERED RUM PUNCH

1 (12-ounce) can pineapple juice
1 cup apple juice
½ cup packed brown sugar
1 teaspoon cinnamon
¼ teaspoon nutmeg
⅛ teaspoon ground cloves
¼ cup butter
1 cup light rum (optional)

1. Combine all ingredients except rum and simmer 15 minutes.

2. Add rum and serve.

**Yields 9 (6-ounce) servings.**

*Double or triple for Christmas parties!*

# ALMOND TEA

6 cups water
1 cup sugar
1 teaspoon vanilla extract
2½ teaspoons almond extract
2 cups strongly brewed tea
Juice of 3 small or 2 large lemons

1. In large saucepan, boil water. Remove from heat and stir in sugar until dissolved.

2. Add vanilla and almond extracts and strongly brewed tea.

3. Squeeze lemon juice into mixture. Serve hot or cold.

**Yields 8 cups.**

# EASY SPICED TEA

2 quarts apple juice
1½ quarts cranberry juice
½ cup brown sugar
4 cinnamon sticks
1 tablespoon whole cloves

1. Pour apple and cranberry juice into large coffee pot.
2. Place brown sugar, cinnamon sticks, and cloves into the coffee filter. Brew as usual.

**Yields 20 (½-cup) servings**

# IRISH CREAM

3 eggs
1 cup sweetened condensed milk
13 ounces rye whiskey
½ pint heavy cream
1½ tablespoons chocolate syrup

1. Beat eggs, add remaining ingredients, and mix well.
2. Store in refrigerator up to several weeks.

**Yields 1 quart.**

*This recipe calls for raw eggs. If concerned about bacterial problems with uncooked egg yolks, avoid or modify this recipe.*

# HIGHWAY DEPARTMENT PUNCH

6 cups heated water
4 cups sugar
5 bananas
Juice of one lemon
1 (46-ounce) can pineapple juice
1 (46-ounce) can orange juice
2 (1-liter) bottles ginger ale

1. Dissolve sugar in heated water. Mash bananas in juice of one lemon. Add pineapple and orange juice. Freeze overnight.
2. Before serving, add ginger ale.

**Yields 40 cups.**

*If frozen in Tupperware, punch stays slushy.*

*Very festive!*

# BREAD, BREAKFAST, & BRUNCH

## Sweet Muffins & Breads

## Easy Breads

## Hard-But-Worth-It Breads

## Side Dishes

## Main Dishes

# APPLESAUCE MUFFINS

1 cup butter or margarine
2 cups sugar
2 eggs
1 cup chopped nuts (optional)
1 tablespoon cinnamon
1 teaspoon nutmeg
2 teaspoons baking soda
1/2 teaspoon salt
4 cups flour
2 cups applesauce

1. Preheat oven to 400°.
2. Cream butter; blend in sugar and eggs.
3. Add nuts and next four ingredients. Mix well. Add flour and applesauce. Mix well.
4. Grease or spray muffin pans and fill each 2/3 full with batter.
5. Bake at 400° for 25 minutes.

**Yields 2 dozen muffins.**

*Batter can be refrigerated up to six weeks. Cooked muffins freeze well.*

# BROUSSARD'S BANANA MUFFINS

1/2 cup vegetable shortening
1 1/2 cups sugar
2 eggs, beaten
2 cups flour
1/4 teaspoon baking soda
1 teaspoon baking powder
1/2 teaspoon salt
1/4 cup milk
1 teaspoon vanilla extract
1 cup mashed bananas

**ICING**

1/3 cup butter
2 cups confectioners' sugar
3 tablespoons bananas
1 tablespoon lemon juice

1. Preheat oven to 350°.
2. For muffins, cream vegetable shortening, sugar, and eggs. Add remaining ingredients, saving bananas to add last.
3. Bake in lightly greased muffin pans at 350° for 15-20 minutes.
4. For icing, beat together all ingredients. Spread onto cooled muffins.

**Yields 2 dozen muffins.**

# ADA'S BANANA BREAD

½ cup shortening
¾ cup sugar
2 eggs
1 teaspoon lemon juice
1 cup mashed bananas
¾ cup sifted flour
1 teaspoon baking soda
½ teaspoon salt
½ cup chopped nuts

1. Preheat oven to 350°.

2. Combine all ingredients well. Pour into a greased and floured 9" x 5" x 3" loaf pan.

3. Bake at 350° for 1 hour. Remove from oven and let stand. After 10 minutes, remove from pan for complete cooling.

**Yields 1 loaf.**

# BANANA-APRICOT BREAD

½ cup vegetable shortening
¾ cup sugar
2 eggs
1 cup mashed ripe bananas
1 teaspoon lemon juice
2 cups all-purpose flour
1 tablespoon baking powder
½ teaspoon salt
¾ cup apricot preserves

1. Preheat oven to 350°.

2. Cream vegetable shortening. Gradually add sugar, beating until light and fluffy. Add eggs one at a time, beating well after each egg.

3. Combine bananas and lemon juice. Add to creamed mixture. Combine flour, baking powder, and salt. Add to mixture, stirring until just moist. Stir in apricot preserves.

4. Spoon batter into 2 greased and floured 8½" x 4½" x 2½" loaf pans. Bake at 350° for 50 minutes until toothpick tests clean.

5. After baking, cool in pans 10 minutes, then remove from pans to cool completely on wire racks.

**Yields 2 loaves.**

# JULIE SAXE'S LEMON-BLUEBERRY BREAD

1 stick butter or margarine, melted
2/3 cup sugar
1 cup low-fat yogurt or sour cream
2 eggs
2 cups flour
1 teaspoon baking powder
1/2 teaspoon baking soda
Zest of one lemon
2 cups blueberries

1. Preheat oven to 375°.
2. Mix butter, sugar, yogurt, and eggs with fork.
3. In larger bowl, combine flour, baking powder, and lemon zest. Add butter mixture with fork.
4. Fold in blueberries. For mini-loaves, bake at 375° for 40-45 minutes. For muffins, bake at 375° for 20-25 minutes.

**Yields 4 mini-loaves or 2 dozen muffins.**

# PLUM NUT BREAD

2 1/2 cups flour
2 cups sugar
2 teaspoons baking soda
1 teaspoon salt
1 teaspoon cinnamon
3 eggs
1 cup buttermilk
1/2 cup vegetable oil
1 teaspoon vanilla extract
1 (4-ounce) jar baby food plums
1 cup chopped pecans

1. Preheat oven to 350°.
2. Mix first 5 dry ingredients.
3. Whisk together eggs, buttermilk, oil, and vanilla, then stir into dry ingredients.
4. Add plums and nuts.
5. Grease and flour 2 loaf pans and fill each with half the batter.
6. Bake at 350° for 1 hour until cake just leaves side of pan.

**Yields 2 loaves.**

# Mom's Pumpkin Bread

1 ¼ cups sugar
½ cup vegetable oil
1 cup pumpkin puree
2 eggs
½ cup water
1 ¾ cups flour
1 teaspoon baking soda
¼ teaspoon baking powder
¼ teaspoon salt
½ teaspoon cinnamon
½ teaspoon allspice
¼ teaspoon ground cloves
½ cup raisins
½ cup chopped nuts

1. Preheat oven to 350°.
2. Beat together sugar, oil, pumpkin, and eggs. Add water.
3. Combine next 7 ingredients. Fold into pumpkin mixture, stirring just to moisten. Fold in raisins and nuts.
4. Pour batter into greased 9" x 5" x 3" loaf pan. Bake at 350° for about 1 hour until toothpick comes out clean.
5. Set pan on rack for 10 minutes, then turn out to cool before cutting.

**Yields 1 loaf.**

# Harvest Loaf

1 cup sugar
½ cup butter
¾ cup pumpkin puree
2 eggs
1 ¾ cups flour
1 teaspoon baking soda
¼ teaspoon baking powder
½ teaspoon salt
2 teaspoons pumpkin pie spice
½ cup chocolate chips
¾ cup chopped walnuts

1. Preheat oven to 350°.
2. Cream sugar, butter, and pumpkin. Add eggs.
3. Combine next 5 ingredients. Fold into pumpkin mixture, stirring just to moisten. Fold in chocolate chips and nuts.
4. Pour batter into greased 9" x 5" x 3" loaf pan. Bake at 350° for 65-70 minutes.
5. Set pan on rack for 10 minutes, then turn out to cool before cutting. Keep refrigerated.

**Yields 1 loaf.**

# POPPY SEED BREAD

3 cups flour
1½ teaspoons baking soda
1 teaspoon salt
1½ tablespoons poppy seeds
3 eggs
2 cups sugar
1½ teaspoons vanilla extract
1½ cups milk
1 cup vegetable oil
½ teaspoon almond extract

**GLAZE**
¾ cup confectioners' sugar
¼ cup orange juice, less for
  thicker glaze
2 tablespoons butter
½ teaspoon almond extract

1. Preheat oven to 350°.
2. Mix first 4 ingredients and set aside.
3. In large mixing bowl, beat eggs. Add sugar and vanilla and beat 1 minute. Stir in milk, alternating with poppy seed mixture. Add oil and almond extract and beat 2 minutes.
4. Grease and flour 9" x 5" x 3" loaf pan. Fill with batter and bake at 350° for 1 hour until toothpick comes out clean.
5. While baking, mix glaze ingredients. Cool bread 10 minutes, then glaze while warm.

**Yields 1 loaf.**

# MARTHA'S CHEESE BREAD

1 cup milk
1 cup butter, melted
2 eggs, well beaten
3 tablespoons grated
  Parmesan cheese
3 cups Bisquick
1 cup sugar
1 cup sour cream
Toasted sesame seeds

1. Preheat oven to 350°.
2. Combine milk and butter. Add eggs and cheese, then stir in Bisquick.
3. Blend sugar and sour cream. Add to batter.
4. Pour batter into greased 13" x 9" x 2" Pyrex pan. Sprinkle with toasted sesame seeds.
5. Bake at 350° for 45 minutes and serve warm.

**Serves 10-12.**

# CREAM CHEESE BRAIDS

1 cup sour cream
½ cup sugar
1 teaspoon salt
½ cup butter, melted
2 (¼-ounce) packages dry
  yeast
½ cup warm water
2 eggs, beaten
4 cups flour

## CREAM CHEESE FILLING

2 (8-ounce) packages cream
  cheese, softened
¾ cup sugar
1 egg, beaten
⅛ teaspoon salt
2 teaspoons vanilla extract

### DAY ONE

1. For bread, heat sour cream over low heat. Stir in sugar, salt and butter, cooling to lukewarm.

2. Sprinkle yeast over warm water in large bowl, stirring until yeast dissolves. Add sour cream mixture, eggs, and flour. Mix well.

3. Cover tightly and refrigerate overnight.

### DAY TWO

1. Preheat oven to 350°.

2. Combine all ingredients for filling.

3. Divide dough into 4 parts. Roll each to an 8" x 12" rectangle on a lightly-floured surface. Spread ¼ of filling on each rectangle. Roll in jelly-roll fashion, beginning at end.

4. Pinch ends together slightly and fold under. Split roll at 2" intervals about two-thirds way through dough. Cover and let rise in warm place for 1 hour until doubled in size.

5. With seam-side down, bake at 350° for 15-20 minutes on greased, long cookie sheet.

6. Let cool, then sprinkle with confectioners' sugar.

**Yields 4 loaves.**

# LAZAR'S LUSCIOUS NUT ROLL

1 (1/4-ounce) package dry
 yeast
1/4 cup lukewarm water
3/4 cup milk, scalded and
 cooled
1/3 cup vegetable shortening
1/3 cup sugar
3/4 teaspoon salt
1 egg
4 cups flour, divided

**FILLING**

4 cups ground walnuts
1/2 cup sugar
3 tablespoons honey
1/2 teaspoon cinnamon
2 eggs
2 1/2 tablespoons milk

1. Preheat oven to 350°.
2. Dissolve yeast in water and set aside.
3. Boil milk and cool. Add vegetable shortening, sugar, salt, egg, and 1 cup flour. Mix with mixer.
4. Add yeast mixture, then remaining 3 cups flour. Knead by hand or with mixer attachment until it leaves side of bowl.
5. Let rise in greased bowl until doubled in size, then divide in half. Roll out each half until paper thin, about 20" x 24".
6. Combine filling ingredients and spread half over each half of dough. Roll in jelly-roll fashion, place on greased cookie sheet, and vent with fork punctures.
7. Bake at 350° for 30-40 minutes. Remove from oven and brush lightly with melted butter.

**Yields about 8 slices per roll.**

# KOLACHY

1 pound butter or margarine
4 cups all-purpose flour
1 (¼-ounce) package dry
yeast
1 cup sour cream
4 egg yolks, beaten
Confectioners' sugar
Flour
Favorite preserves

1. Preheat oven to 350°.

2. Cut butter into flour. Dissolve yeast in sour cream and add egg yolks. Stir into flour mixture, knead well, and refrigerate until well chilled.

3. Cover pastry board with sugar and flour. Roll out dough to ¼" and cut into 2-4" squares. Fill with preserves. Pinch corners or roll up.

4. Place on greased cookie sheet and bake at 350° for 15 minutes until brown.

**Yields 4-5 dozen.**

*Great holiday gift.*

# SCHNECHEN (LITTLE SWEET CAKES)

2 cups flour
½ pound butter
½ pound cream cheese
**FILLING**
2 tablespoons cinnamon
6 tablespoons sugar
½ cup chopped walnuts
½ cup chopped golden raisins

1. Preheat oven to 350°.

2. Combine first 3 ingredients, wrap in wax paper, and refrigerate overnight.

3. Roll out dough on floured board in batches. Cut in circles with medium-sized cookie cutter, then roll each circle once to ⅛" thick.

4. Combine filling ingredients and place ½ tablespoon on each circle. Bend into crescent shapes.

5. Place on ungreased cookie sheet and bake at 350° for 20-30 minutes.

**Yields 2 dozen.**

*Freezes well.*

# Apricot-Pineapple Kugel (Noodle Pudding)

1 (16-ounce) package
  medium egg noodles
¼ pound margarine
6 large eggs, well beaten
¾ cup sugar
½ teaspoon salt
1 (20-ounce) can crushed
  pineapple with juice
1 (29-ounce) can apricot
  halves, drained and divided
1 (12-ounce) jar apricot
  preserves, divided
Cinnamon to taste
Sugar to taste

1. Preheat oven to 375°.

2. Cook noodles according to package and drain. Add margarine to melt in hot noodles.

3. Add eggs, sugar, salt, pineapple with juice, half the apricot halves, and half the preserves. Mix well after each addition.

4. Pour into greased 13" x 9" x 2" baking dish. Place remaining apricot halves, cut side down, on noodle mixture.

5. Dot with remaining preserves and sprinkle with cinnamon and sugar. Bake at 375° for 1 hour.

**Serves 10.**

# NOODLE CHARLOTTE

1 (16-ounce) package
  medium egg noodles
½ pound margarine
1 cup sugar
6 eggs, separated
1 (8-ounce) package cream
  cheese, softened
1 (16-ounce) container
  cottage cheese
1 (16-ounce) carton sour
  cream
1 teaspoon vanilla extract
Raisins (optional)

## TOPPING

½ cup corn flake crumbs
¼ cup sugar
1 teaspoon cinnamon
4 tablespoons margarine,
  melted

1. Preheat oven to 350°.

2. Cook noodles according to package and drain.

3. Cream margarine, sugar, and egg yolks. Add next 5 ingredients. Stir into noodles.

4. Beat egg whites until stiff. Fold into noodle mixture and pour into greased 13" x 9" x 2" baking dish. Bake at 350° for 40-45 minutes.

5. Prepare topping by combining all 4 ingredients well.

6. Remove noodle mixture from oven and sprinkle with topping. Return to oven and bake 10 more minutes.

**Serves 15-20.**

*Can be frozen.*

# CINNAMON RAISIN CUSTARD

16 slices cinnamon raisin
bread, trimmed
1 stick butter, melted
4 eggs
2 egg yolks
3/4 cup sugar
1 cup cream
3 cups milk
1 tablespoon vanilla or
brandy extract
Cinnamon

1. Preheat oven to 350°.

2. Slice bread to fit neatly in a
buttered 13" x 9" x 2" pan.
Arrange slices in pan, overlap-
ping if necessary, and brush
generously with melted butter.

3. Combine remaining ingredients
except cinnamon and pour over
bread. Sprinkle with cinnamon.

4. Place in pan of hot water and
bake at 350° for 40-45 minutes
until puffy and lightly browned.
Let cool 15 minutes before
slicing.

**Serves 10-12.**

*Can assemble night before,
refrigerate, and bake next day.*

# MONKEY BREAD

2 cans biscuits
1 cup chopped pecans
1 stick butter, cut into small
pieces
1 cup brown sugar
1/2 cup sugar
2 teaspoons cinnamon

1. Preheat oven to 350°.

2. Cut each biscuit into four pieces.

3. Mix remaining ingredients. Add
biscuits and stir.

4. Bake at 350° for 30 minutes in
ungreased 9" x 3" Bundt pan.

5. Flip over on serving plate and
serve immediately.

**Serves 6-8.**

# GRANNY ROUX'S DILLY BREAD

2 cups unsifted flour
2 tablespoons sugar
1 teaspoon salt
1 tablespoon instant minced onion
2 tablespoons dill seed
¼ tablespoon baking soda
1 (¼-ounce) package dry yeast
1 tablespoon margarine or butter, softened
¼ cup hot tap water
¼ cup creamed cottage cheese
1 egg, room temperature

1. Preheat oven to 350°.

2. Combine ¼ cup flour and next 6 ingredients. Add margarine.

3. Add hot tap water and beat 2 minutes at medium speed. Add cottage cheese, egg, and ½ cup flour. Beat 2 minutes at high speed.

4. Knead in remaining 1 to 1¼ cups flour to make stiff batter.

5. Cover and let rise about 30 minutes until doubled in size. Punch down and turn into greased 1½-quart casserole dish or 9" x 5" x 3" loaf pan. Cover and let rise about 50 minutes until doubled in size again.

6. Bake at 350° for 30 minutes. Remove from pan and cool on wire rack.

**Serves 6-8.**

*Great with gumbo on a cold day.*

# Mexican Cornbread

4 tablespoons jalapeño
   pepper juice
3¼ cups corn-muffin mix
2½ cups milk
½ cup corn oil
3 eggs
1 teaspoon salt
3 teaspoons sugar
1½ cups diced pasteurized
   processed cheese
1 onion, finely chopped
   (optional)
1 (17-ounce) can mexi-corn
   or regular canned corn

1. Preheat oven to 375°.
2. Combine all ingredients with a fork.
3. Pour into 13" x 9" x 2" casserole dish and bake at 375° for 45 minutes.

**Yields 10 servings.**

# Patsy's Cornbread

½ cup chopped, sautéed
   onion
½ cup grated Cheddar cheese
1 egg
½ cup milk
1 (8½-ounce) box cornbread
   mix

**Topping**

½ cup grated Cheddar cheese
2 tablespoons melted butter
1 tablespoon poppy seeds

1. Preheat oven to 400°.
2. Combine ingredients for cornbread and pour into greased 9" x 9" x 2" pan.
3. Combine topping ingredients and place on cornbread.
4. Bake at 400° for 20-25 minutes.

**Serves 12.**

*Great with a bowl of beans.*

# CHEESE GARLIC BISCUITS

2 cups Bisquick
²/₃ cup milk
½ cup shredded Cheddar
  cheese
**TOPPING**
¼ cup margarine, melted
¼ teaspoon garlic powder

1. Preheat oven to 450°.
2. Mix Bisquick, milk, and cheese, beating until dough is soft.
3. Spoon drop onto ungreased cookie sheet and bake at 450° for 8-10 minutes until golden brown.
4. For topping, combine margarine and garlic powder and brush onto finished biscuits.

**Yields 1 dozen biscuits.**

*Can add cooked bacon bits to batter.*

# JALAPEÑO CHEESE GRITS

2 cups milk
1 cup water
1 cup instant grits
2 tablespoons butter
1 jalapeño pepper, seeded
  and minced
2 teaspoons Worcestershire
  sauce
2 teaspoons minced garlic
1 teaspoon black pepper
Dash of Tabasco sauce
Salt
12 ounces Monterey Jack with
  jalapeño peppers, shredded

1. Combine all ingredients except cheese in heavy, medium saucepan and cook about 30 minutes over medium-high heat, stirring frequently, until thickened.
2. Add cheese and cook about 10 minutes until consistency of soft mashed potatoes.
3. Transfer grits to bowl and serve hot.

**Serves 4-6.**

*Great with roast chicken or lamb.*

# BAKED CHEESE & GARLIC GRITS

1 cup grits
Salt, onion salt, and garlic
  powder to taste
2 cups shredded Cheddar
  cheese
1 cup half-and-half
4 eggs, separated and beaten
Dash of Tabasco sauce
2 tablespoons butter
1/2 cup chopped green onions
Paprika for topping

1. Preheat oven to 325°.

2. In large saucepan, cook grits according to package directions in water seasoned with salt, onion salt, and garlic powder.

3. In small saucepan, heat cheese and half-and-half. Add to cooked grits.

4. Add egg yolks, then egg whites. Add dash of Tabasco sauce. Beat mixture lightly and add butter.

5. Pour into ungreased loaf pan or 13" x 9" x 2" casserole dish and bake at 325° for 1 hour until firm.

6. Top with green onions, paprika, and sprinkle of shredded cheese. Serve as side dish.

**Serves 6-8.**

*Not for the calorie or cholesterol conscious!*

# CATHY'S QUICK POPOVERS

2 eggs
1 cup flour
1 cup milk
1/2 teaspoon salt

1. Preheat oven to 450°.

2. Beat eggs and add remaining ingredients.

3. Fill greased muffin tins 1/2 full.

4. Bake at 450° for 20 minutes. Reduce heat to 350° and bake another 20 minutes.

**Yields 6 popovers.**

# SUNDAY MORNING MICROWAVE EGGS

6-8 eggs
¼ pound Cheddar cheese, grated
⅛-¼ cup milk
½ teaspoon garlic salt
1 teaspoon dill

1. Whisk eggs in 1½-quart microwaveable bowl. Add remaining ingredients.

2. Microwave on medium-high power for 10 minutes until firm, rotating and stirring every 3 minutes.

**Serves 4-6.**

*Ham and green peppers make tasty additions.*

# FAVORITE EGG CASSEROLE

6-8 eggs, slightly beaten
1 pint cottage cheese
¾-1 pound Cheddar or Monterey Jack cheese, grated
1 cup Bisquick
1 stick butter or margarine, melted
1 cup milk
8 ounces cubed ham (optional)
1 tablespoon dried parsley flakes
Salt and pepper to taste

1. Preheat oven to 350°.

2. Combine all ingredients and pour into greased 13" x 9" x 2" baking dish.

3. Bake at 350° for 40-50 minutes.

**Serves 10-12.**

*Substitute cooked bacon or sausage for ham.*

# CHILI 'N CHEESE BREAKFAST CASSEROLE

3 English muffins, split
2 tablespoons butter, softened
1 pound pork sausage
1 (4-ounce) can chopped
  green chilies, drained
3 cups shredded Cheddar
  cheese
1½ cups sour cream
12 eggs, beaten

1. Spread cut side of English muffins with 1 teaspoon butter. Place buttered side down in lightly greased 13" x 9" x 2" baking dish.

2. In a separate skillet, brown sausage, stirring to crumble. Drain.

3. Layer over English muffins half of sausage, chilies, and cheese. Whisk sour cream and eggs, then pour over casserole.

4. Layer again with remaining sausage, chilies, and cheese.

5. Cover and refrigerate 8 hours.

6. Preheat oven to 350°. Let casserole stand at room temperature for 30 minutes. Then bake at 350° for 35-40 minutes.

**Serves 8-10.**

*Make ahead and freeze; thaw; then bake as usual.*

*Great with spicy vegetable juice!*

# MEXICAN BREAKFAST CASSEROLE

1 pound sausage
6 eggs
2 cups milk
1 teaspoon salt
1 teaspoon dry mustard
Crust of 6 slices bread
1 (4-ounce) can chopped
  green chilies
1 teaspoon chopped jalapeño
  peppers (optional)
1 cup grated Cheddar cheese

1.  Brown sausage, drain, and cool.
2.  Beat eggs. Add milk, salt, mustard, then beat again.
3.  Add remaining ingredients and mix thoroughly. Pour into greased 13" x 9" x 2" casserole dish and let set overnight.
4.  Preheat oven to 350° and bake for 45 minutes.

**Serves 8-10.**

# BREAKFAST SAUSAGE RING

2 pounds ground sausage
2 eggs, beaten
2 cups saltine cracker crumbs
  (about 1 stack crumbled)
1½ cups peeled and finely
  chopped green apples

1.  Preheat oven to 350°.
2.  Combine all ingredients, mixing well with hands.
3.  Shape into 10" ring and place on broiler pan.
4.  Bake at 350° for 1 hour. Slice thinly and serve hot.

**Yields 20 thin slices.**

*Serve with crackers as an appetizer.*

# BUTTERMILK PANCAKES

1 egg, slightly beaten
½ cup milk
1 cup buttermilk
1 teaspoon soda
½ teaspoon salt
1 tablespoon sugar
2 tablespoons cornmeal
2 tablespoons oil
Flour to thicken (about ¾ cup)

1. Combine all ingredients except flour in order given.

2. Lightly mix in enough flour to make a thin, lumpy batter. Let sit for 5-10 minutes.

3. Heat lightly greased griddle or skillet to medium high. Pour batter, thinned with milk if needed, into separate pancakes.

4. Flip when top of pancake is bubbled and leave in skillet for another 1-2 minutes.

**Serves 4.**

# CHALLAH FRENCH TOAST

1 large Challah (plain or raisin)
8 eggs
3 cups milk
¼ cup sugar
1 tablespoon vanilla extract
1 teaspoon salt
Cinnamon
Sugar
Raisin or currants
Maple syrup (optional)

1. Cut Challah lengthwise (sandwich style) and then into 2" squares. Place tightly side by side into greased 13" x 9" x 2" pan to make bottom layer.

2. Mix remaining ingredients and pour on top of Challah. Refrigerate overnight or up to 3 days.

3. When ready to cook, preheat oven to 350°. Dot Challah with margarine and sprinkle with cinnamon, sugar, and raisins or currants.

4. Bake at 350° for 45 minutes. Serve with maple syrup.

**Serves 10.**

*Easy and out-of-this-world delicious!*

# DAY BEFORE FRENCH TOAST

6 slices French or Italian-style bread, cut in ¾" slices
3 eggs
1 cup milk
3 tablespoons sugar
¼ teaspoon salt
½ teaspoon cinnamon
¼ teaspoon nutmeg
1 teaspoon vanilla extract
2 tablespoons butter
Fresh fruit or maple syrup for topping

1. Arrange bread slices in single layer in 13" x 9" x 2" baking dish.

2. Combine next six ingredients, beating until smooth.

3. Pour mixture over bread and turn slices to coat evenly. Cover and refrigerate overnight.

4. When ready to cook, melt butter in skillet. Remove bread from egg mixture and sauté about 5 minutes on each side until golden.

5. Sprinkle with confectioners' sugar and top with fresh fruit or syrup.

**Serves 2-3.**

*Easily doubled.*

# SOUPS, SALADS, & SANDWICHES

# Cajun Broccoli-Cauliflower Soup

1 stick butter (1/2 cup)
1 large onion, chopped
3 garlic cloves, minced
6 parsley sprigs, chopped
2 (8-ounce) packages cream
  cheese
7 cups water, divided
8 chicken bouillon cubes
1 large bunch broccoli, cut
  into bite-sized pieces
1 large bunch cauliflower, cut
  into bite-sized pieces
Salt and pepper to taste
Hot pepper sauce
4 tablespoons shallots

1.  In 5-quart saucepan, melt butter
    and sauté onion, garlic, and
    parsley for about 3 minutes.

2.  In blender, puree cream cheese
    with 2 cups water. Add to
    sautéed vegetables in pan.

3.  Stir in 5 remaining cups water
    and bouillon cubes. Add broc-
    coli, cauliflower, salt, pepper,
    and hot sauce to taste.

4.  Simmer about 20-30 minutes
    and add shallots 5 minutes
    before serving.

**Serves 8.**

*Puree in blender for thick and
creamy soup.*

# Texas Potato Soup

4 cups peeled and diced raw
  potatoes
1 1/2 cups water
1/2 cup chopped onion
1/2 cup chopped celery
1 tablespoon chicken
  bouillon granules
2 cups milk, divided
1 (8-ounce) carton sour cream
2 tablespoons flour
2 tablespoons chopped chives
Salt and pepper to taste

1.  Combine potatoes, water, onion,
    celery, and bouillon in small
    Dutch oven. Simmer 20 minutes.

2.  Mix in 1 cup milk and sour
    cream. Add flour, stir well, then
    add remaining milk.

3.  Add chives, salt, and pepper.
    Simmer 15 minutes, then serve.

**Serves 4-6.**

# ELLIE'S GINGER PEA SOUP

1 (10-ounce) package frozen
  peas
1 1" piece fresh ginger,
  peeled and sliced
3 tablespoons quick cooking
  Cream of Wheat
½ cup water
2 cups chicken broth
Milk to thin

1. In a 3-quart saucepan, cook three-fourths of the peas according to package directions with half of the ginger. Reserve one-fourth frozen peas to add later.

2. Add Cream of Wheat and water to cooked peas and cook another few minutes.

3. Add chicken broth and remaining peas and ginger.

4. Puree all in blender. Strain mixture into bowl in order to remove pea skins. Add milk to thin to desired consistency. Serve warm or chilled.

**Serves 3.**

# SPICED PLUM SOUP

4 (16-ounce) cans plums in
  syrup
1 bottle Burgundy wine
1 teaspoon ground cinnamon
½ teaspoon ground nutmeg
½ teaspoon ground cloves
2 tablespoons sugar
¼ cup Cointreau orange
  liqueur
Zest of 2 lemons
Sour cream for garnish
8 sprigs fresh mint for garnish

1. Drain and pit plums, reserving syrup.

2. In medium pot, combine plums, syrup from plums, and next five ingredients. Bring mixture to boil, then reduce heat. Simmer for 30 minutes

3. In blender, puree soup in small batches until smooth. Strain into bowl.

4. Add Cointreau and lemon zest. Mix well.

5. Serve hot or cold. Garnish with dollop of sour cream and mint sprig.

**Serves 8.**

# LOUISE'S PUMPKIN SOUP

3 large onions, chopped
¼ cup butter
1½ teaspoons curry powder
6 cups canned pumpkin
2 teaspoons salt
7½ cups chicken broth, divided
1 cup milk
1 cup heavy cream

1. In 6-8 quart stock pot, sauté onion in butter. Add curry and sauté 2 minutes more.

2. Add pumpkin, salt, and 3½ cups of chicken broth. Simmer about 10 minutes. Puree in blender or food processor.

3. Add remaining broth, milk, and cream while processing. (May need to process in batches.) Return to stock pot and heat, but do not boil.

**Serves 10-12.**

*Healthy hint: reduce fat by using less butter, fat free chicken broth, and low-fat milk.*

# CREAM OF ZUCCHINI SOUP

4 medium zucchini, grated
1 teaspoon salt
¾ cup butter
4 medium carrots, grated
1 medium onion, chopped
8 tablespoons flour
2 (13½-ounce) cans chicken broth
8 ounces Monterey Jack cheese, grated
½ cup half-and-half
1½ teaspoons pepper
1½ teaspoons garlic salt
Salt to taste

1. Place grated zucchini in colander, sprinkle with salt and let stand for 30 minutes.

2. Press zucchini between paper towels.

3. Heat butter in frying pan and sauté zucchini, carrots, and onion until slightly limp.

4. Stir in flour and cook over low heat for 5 minutes. Add broth and stir until smooth.

5. Add cheese and stir until melted, then add remaining ingredients and simmer for 30 minutes.

**Serves 6-8.**

# PENNSYLVANIA DUTCH SQUASH SOUP

4 tablespoons butter
2 cups chopped onions
3 medium butternut squash
3 medium Granny Smith
  apples
3 cups chicken broth
1 cup whipping cream
2 tablespoons brandy
2 tablespoons curry powder
Salt and white pepper to taste

1. Melt butter in heavy, large saucepan. Add onions and cook over low heat for 20 minutes until tender.

2. Cut squash in half lengthwise. Remove seeds, peel, and chop.

3. Peel, core, and chop apples.

4. Add squash, apples, and remaining ingredients (except salt and pepper) to onions.

5. Simmer (do not boil) in covered saucepan for 30 minutes until squash and apples are tender.

6. Strain mixture, saving both liquids and solids. Puree solids in blender or food processor until smooth.

7. Return all ingredients to large saucepan and stir until smooth.

8. Season with salt and pepper and continue to simmer until ready to serve.

**Serves 8.**

*Heating squash in microwave makes peeling easier.*

*Hearty entrée with whole grain bread and cheese. Freezes well in quart freezer bags (2 servings per bag).*

# VEGETABLE GUMBO

1 tablespoon olive or canola
oil
1 garlic clove, finely chopped
1/4 cup chopped bell pepper
1/4 cup chopped onion
1 celery stalk, chopped
1 cup water or chicken broth
(more if needed)
1 (16-ounce) can whole
peeled tomatoes
1 (16-ounce) package frozen
vegetable soup mix
1/2 teaspoon salt
1/2 teaspoon black pepper
1/4 teaspoon garlic powder
Cayenne to taste
3 tablespoons butter or
margarine
3 tablespoons flour
1-1 1/2 cups chopped, cooked
turkey or chicken (optional)

1. Heat oil in medium-sized pan over low heat.

2. Add garlic, bell pepper, onion, and celery. Sauté until onions are translucent, then set aside.

3. In medium saucepan, bring water and tomatoes to boil. Break up tomatoes.

4. Add vegetable soup mix, salt, pepper, garlic powder, and cayenne. Cover and return to boil.

5. Reduce heat, add sautéed ingredients, and simmer 10 minutes.

6. Make roux by melting butter in saucepan, adding flour, and stirring until golden brown.

7. Stir roux into mixture and add turkey or chicken if desired. Cook 5 minutes, stirring occasionally, until tender.

8. Serve hot over rice.

**Serves 4.**

*Vegetable soup mix includes potatoes, carrots, green beans, corn, lima beans, green peas, celery, okra, and onions.*

# TEXAS TURKEY GUMBO

Leftover Thanksgiving turkey
2-3 bouillon cubes
2 tablespoons margarine
2 tablespoons flour
1 large onion, chopped
1 bell pepper, chopped
2 celery stalks, chopped
2 tablespoons chopped
   parsley
2 garlic cloves, minced
Thyme to taste
Salt and pepper to taste
1 pound smoke sausage or
   andouille
1 (10-ounce) package frozen
   okra, sliced
1 pint oysters (optional)

1. Remove turkey meat from bone.

2. In large pot, cover bones with water, add bouillon cubes, and boil until bones fall apart.

3. Remove bones from turkey stock and add turkey meat. Set aside.

4. Make roux by melting margarine in saucepan, adding flour, and whisking about 5 minutes to a golden brown paste.

5. Add onions and next 4 ingredients to roux, then add 1 cup of turkey stock. Cook down until vegetables are tender.

6. Add thyme, salt, and pepper to stock, then simmer for 2 hours.

7. Add sausage, okra, and oysters, and simmer 5-10 more minutes.

8. Serve hot over rice.

**Serves 8-10.**

*Substitute chicken for turkey.*

# AUNT B.B.'S SHRIMP GUMBO

½ cup flour
⅓ cup oil
2 cups chopped white onion
½ cup chopped green onions
½ cup chopped parsley
2 garlic cloves, minced
1½ quarts water
1 tablespoon salt
1 teaspoon pepper
½ teaspoon cayenne
2 pounds shrimp, shelled and deveined
1 tablespoon filé (optional)

1. In heavy skillet, combine flour and oil. Cook over medium heat 25-35 minutes to a dark reddish-brown roux. Stir frequently first 15 minutes and constantly last 10-20 minutes.

2. Add white onion and sauté until translucent. Add green onions and sauté until limp.

3. Add next 6 ingredients and simmer for 45 minutes more.

4. Add shrimp and cook 5-10 minutes until shrimp turns pink. Sprinkle with filé. Serve over rice with Granny Roux's Dilly Bread.

**Serves 8.**

# GAZPACHO

4 cups tomato or spicy vegetable juice
1 small onion, minced
2 cups diced fresh tomato
1 cup minced green pepper
1 garlic clove, minced
1 cucumber, diced
2 green onions, chopped
¼ cup chopped parsley
1 teaspoon honey
Juice of ½ lemon
Juice of 1 lime
2 tablespoons wine vinegar
2 tablespoons olive oil
Dash of cumin
Dash of Tabasco sauce
Salt and pepper to taste

1. Combine all ingredients in a large bowl.

2. Chill and serve.

**Yields 8-10 cups.**

# SNAPPY TORTILLA SOUP

4 large chicken breasts
8 cups water
Onion, carrot, celery, salt, and pepper to flavor stock
2 tablespoons oil
1 medium onion, chopped
2 garlic cloves, minced
1 (4-ounce) can chopped green chilies
1 (28-ounce) can crushed tomatoes
2 teaspoons Worcestershire sauce
2 tablespoons cumin
1 tablespoon chili powder
1 teaspoon salt
1/4 teaspoon black pepper
2 yellow squash, thinly sliced
2 zucchini squash, thinly sliced

**GARNISH**

Corn tortillas, cut in strips and toasted
4 ounces Cheddar cheese, grated
Avocado slices
Cilantro (optional)

1. In stock pot, boil chicken in water flavored with onion, carrots, celery, salt, and pepper. Remove chicken, cool, and dice.

2. Refrigerate chicken stock, cool, skim off fat, and add chicken pieces.

3. Heat oil in skillet and sauté onion, garlic, and green chilies. Add to stock pot.

4. Add next 8 ingredients and simmer for 30 minutes.

5. Drop tortilla strips in soup bowls. Pour in soup and garnish with grated cheese, avocado, and cilantro.

**Serves 6-8.**

*For extra spice, add a few shakes of red cayenne pepper.*

# MEATBALL SOUP

## MEATBALLS

3/4 pound lean ground beef
1/3 cup seasoned dry bread crumbs
1 egg
2 tablespoons grated Parmesan cheese
2 tablespoons finely chopped parsley
1/4 teaspoon pepper
1/4 teaspoon garlic powder

## SOUP

1 tablespoon olive oil
1 1/4 cups chopped onion
1 (13 3/4-ounce) can beef broth
1 cup water
1 (35-ounce) can whole tomatoes, chopped
1 teaspoon basil
1 teaspoon oregano
1/2 teaspoon sugar
1 (10-ounce) package frozen green beans
3/4 cup uncooked 1/4" pasta tubes
Grated Parmesan cheese

1. For meatballs, combine ingredients with fork and shape into 1" balls. Set aside.

2. For soup, heat oil in Dutch oven or stock pot and cook onion 3-5 minutes until soft.

3. Stir in beef broth, water, tomatoes with liquid, basil, oregano, and sugar. Bring to boil over high heat, then lower heat and simmer for 8 minutes.

4. Add green beans and simmer 5 minutes.

5. Stir in pasta and carefully add meatballs. Simmer 15 more minutes, stirring occasionally, until pasta and meatballs are cooked.

6. Serve with grated Parmesan cheese.

**Serves 6-8.**

*Fun to make and eat with children.*

# RUSSIAN BORSCHT

3-4 pounds beef and beef
  bones for stock
1 head green cabbage, halved
2 pounds fresh beets,
  destalked
Margarine for sautéing
2-3 carrots, sliced
1 pound parsnips or turnips,
  sliced
1 pound onions, chopped
1 (35-ounce) can Italian
  peeled tomatoes
4 beef bouillon cubes
Salt to taste
Sugar to taste
Sour cream and fresh
  chopped dill for garnish

## DAY 1

1. Make strong beef broth by covering meat, bone, and half of cabbage with water in stock pot. Cook until meat is tender.

2. Remove meat and set aside. Remove bones and half of cabbage and discard.

3. Boil down broth, then refrigerate overnight.

4. Trim and cube meat. Refrigerate overnight.

5. Roast or steam beets until tender. Peel and slice, then refrigerate overnight.

## DAY 2

1. Skim fat off broth, then reheat broth.

2. Sauté carrots and parsnips for 5 minutes, then add onions for 2 minutes more until wilted.

3. Add sautéed mixture, tomatoes, and beets to broth.

4. Cut remaining half of cabbage into 1" slices. Add to broth.

5. If needed to cover vegetables, add extra broth of 4 bouillon cubes to 4 cups water.

6. Add meat to soup and season to taste with salt and sugar. Garnish with sour cream and fresh dill.

**Serves 12.**

*Tastes even better the next day!*

# CRANBERRY MOLD

4 cups whole raw cranberries
1½ cups chopped walnuts
2 cups chopped celery
¾ cup sugar
1 (6-ounce) package
   strawberry-flavored gelatin
3 cups boiling water
2 tablespoons lemon juice

1. In food processor, finely chop cranberries and walnuts. Add celery.

2. In 13" x 9" x 2" baking dish or ring mold, dissolve gelatin in water and lemon juice. When gelatin begins to thicken, stir in cranberry mixture.

3. Chill before serving.

**Serves 15.**

*Garnish with holly for the holidays.*

# FRUIT FLUFF

2 cups raw cranberries,
   ground
3 cups tiny marshmallows
¾ cup sugar
2 cups diced tart apples
½ cup seedless green grapes,
   sliced in half
½ cup broken walnuts
¼ teaspoon salt
1 cup heavy cream, whipped

1. Combine first 3 ingredients and chill overnight.

2. Next day, add remaining ingredients, mix well, and chill.

**Serves 12.**

# HIDDEN TREASURE SALAD

1 (3-ounce) package
strawberry-flavored gelatin
1 cup boiling water
1 (10-ounce) package frozen
strawberries, partially
thawed
1 (15¼-ounce) can crushed
pineapple, drained
3 medium bananas, mashed
½ cup chopped pecans
1 (8-ounce) container sour
cream

1. Dissolve gelatin in water. Stir in fruit and pecans.

2. Grease 12" x 8" x 2" dish and pour in half the gelatin mixture. Chill.

3. Cover chilled gelatin mixture with sour cream and top with remaining gelatin mixture. Chill before serving.

**Serves 12.**

# MANGO MOLD

2½ cups boiling water
1 (3-ounce) package orange-
flavored gelatin
2 (3-ounce) package lemon-
flavored gelatin
1 (29-ounce) can mangoes
with juice
1 (8-ounce) package cream
cheese
¼ cup lemon juice

1. In blender or food processor, dissolve gelatins in boiling water.

2. Add mangoes with juice, cream cheese, and lemon juice. Blend well.

3. Transfer to 13" x 9" x 2" baking dish or ring mold and refrigerate until firm.

**Serves 12-15.**

# JERSEY TOMATOES WITH HERB DRESSING

## DRESSING
⅔ cup extra virgin olive oil
⅓ cup balsamic vinegar
1 teaspoon Dijon mustard
1 garlic clove, minced
2 tablespoons chopped fresh
  parsley
2 tablespoons chopped fresh
  basil
Fresh basil leaves for garnish

## SALAD
4 ripe tomatoes, thinly sliced
2 shallots, chopped

1. Combine dressing ingredients in container with tight fitting lid. Shake until well blended. Refrigerate until ready to use.

2. Arrange sliced tomatoes on serving platter and pour dressing over them.

3. Sprinkle with shallots and garnish with fresh basil leaves.

**Serves 4-6.**

*Any ripe, red, luscious tomato is delicious with this dressing.*

*Slices of fresh mozzarella make a wonderful addition.*

# JODIE'S CAULIFLOWER & BROCCOLI SALAD

1 head cauliflower
1 bunch broccoli
1 small bunch green onions

## DRESSING
1 (8-ounce) carton sour cream
½ cup mayonnaise
¼ cup sugar
2 tablespoons fresh lemon
  juice
¼ teaspoon salt

1. Wash vegetables and cut into small pieces.

2. Mix dressing ingredients and pour over vegetables.

3. Chill at least 1 hour before serving.

**Serves 10-12.**

# Mrs. Bolton's Broccoli Salad

**SALAD**

1 large bunch broccoli, cut in
small pieces
½ pound bacon, fried and
crumbled
½ medium red onion,
chopped
1 cup sunflower seeds
½ cup raisins

**DRESSING**

2 tablespoons cider vinegar
1 cup mayonnaise
¼ cup sugar

1. Mix salad ingredients in large
bowl.
2. Mix dressing ingredients and
pour over salad.
3. Refrigerate 2-4 hours, then serve.

**Serves 8.**

# Spinach Salad

**DRESSING**

¾ cup vegetable oil
¼ cup red wine vinegar
2 garlic cloves, minced
½ teaspoon salt
½ teaspoon pepper
¼ cup Dijon mustard
¼ cup stone-ground mustard
¼ cup maple syrup

**SALAD**

1 (12-ounce) package spinach
5 large mushrooms, sliced
1 small red onion, finely
chopped
6 strips bacon, cooked and
crumbled
2 hard-boiled eggs, chopped
coarsely

1. Whisk dressing ingredients
together.
2. Combine salad ingredients and
toss with dressing.

**Serves 4.**

# Westport Room Salad

## Dressing

1 cup mayonnaise
2 teaspoons grated Parmesan
  cheese
1 teaspoon lemon juice
1 garlic clove, minced
Salt and pepper to taste

## Salad

1 head Romaine lettuce
1/2 cup grated cauliflower
1 cup buttered bread crumbs

1. Combine dressing ingredients.
2. Wash and dry lettuce completely. Break into pieces and toss with dressing.
3. Sprinkle grated cauliflower and bread crumbs over salad, but do not toss again. Serve immediately.

**Serves 6-8.**

# Caesar Salad

## Dressing

1 garlic clove, minced
1/2 cup vegetable oil
2 tablespoons lemon juice
1/2 cup grated Parmesan
  cheese
1 teaspoon Worcestershire
  sauce
1/2 teaspoon salt
1/2 teaspoon pepper

## Salad

1 head Romaine lettuce
1 cup croutons

1. In food processor or blender, blend dressing ingredients in order given. Chill well.
2. Wash and dry lettuce completely. Break into pieces and toss with dressing. Top with croutons.

**Serves 6-8.**

**Yields 1 cup of dressing.**

*Leftover dressing is great on hamburgers.*

# Gram's Coleslaw

## Dressing

½-¾ cup mayonnaise
2-3 tablespoons milk
2 tablespoons sugar
1 tablespoon vinegar
1 tablespoon dried onion
1 teaspoon celery seed
¼-½ teaspoon dry mustard

## Salad

1 medium head cabbage
2 carrots, peeled and cut in 3"
    pieces
½ green pepper, minced

1. Combine dressing ingredients and set aside.

2. Shred cabbage and carrots in food processor. Mince green pepper and add to cabbage and carrots.

3. Toss salad with dressing. If too dry, add mayonnaise one tablespoon at a time.

4. Refrigerate 2 hours to let flavors marry.

**Serves 6.**

# Cabbage Ramen Salad

1 (3-ounce) package chicken-flavored Ramen noodle soup

## Dressing

½ cup oil
3 tablespoons white vinegar
2 tablespoons sugar
Ramen seasoning packet
Pepper to taste

## Salad

Ramen noodles, crumbled
½ cup sliced almonds
½ cup sunflower seeds
1 medium cabbage, chopped
1 bunch green onions,
    chopped

1. Combine dressing ingredients and mix well. Set aside.

2. Mix dry, crumbled noodles with almonds and seeds in zip-lock bag.

3. When ready to serve, add noodle mixture to cabbage and onions in large salad bowl. Toss well with dressing.

**Serves 8-10.**

# SOUTHEAST TEXAS HOT POTATO SALAD

6-8 medium potatoes, boiled, peeled, and diced
1 pound pasteurized processed cheese, diced
1 cup real mayonnaise
½ cup chopped onion
Salt and pepper to taste
½ pound bacon, fried, drained, and crumbled (or artificial bacon)
2 tablespoons sweet pickle relish

1. Preheat oven to 325°.
2. Toss potatoes with cheese, mayonnaise, onion, and seasonings. Turn into buttered 13" x 9" x 2" baking dish.
3. Combine bacon and relish. Spread over potato mixture.
4. Bake at 325° for 45 minutes until thoroughly heated.

**Serves 10.**

*Can prepare ahead and refrigerate, allowing 15 minutes additional cooking time.*

# SWEET & SOUR POTATO SALAD

**DRESSING**
1½ cups mayonnaise
¼ cup evaporated milk
¼ cup vinegar
3-4 tablespoons sugar
¼ cup vegetable oil
1 teaspoon mustard
Salt, pepper, and garlic powder to taste

**SALAD**
6-8 potatoes, boiled and chopped
6 eggs, boiled and chopped
2 stalks celery, finely chopped
1 large onion, finely chopped
2 dill pickles, chopped
½ cup sweet pickle relish
1 (2-ounce) can pimentos, chopped
Sliced olives (optional)

1. Blend dressing ingredients until smooth, adjusting sugar and vinegar to taste. Set aside.
2. Mix salad ingredients together in large bowl and toss with dressing.

**Serves 8-10.**

# WARM PEPPERED BACON SALAD

½ pound thickly sliced peppered bacon, cut in ½" pieces
1 cup pecans
1 pound mushrooms (domestic or part domestic/part shiitake), sliced
⅓ cup balsamic vinegar
Salt and pepper to taste
4-6 cups salad greens (such as Boston, Romaine, spinach, radicchio, etc.)
½ cup sliced green onions

1. In large skillet, cook bacon over medium heat until brown and crisp. Remove bacon and drain on paper towel. Reserve bacon grease in skillet.

2. Sauté pecans in bacon grease for 1-2 minutes. Remove, drain, and set aside for topping.

3. Add mushrooms to skillet and cook over low heat until soft.

4. Stir in cooked bacon and vinegar. Add salt and pepper to taste and cook until warmed through.

5. Wash and cut up salad greens and toss with warm bacon mixture.

6. Top with toasted pecans and sliced green onions.

**Serves 6-8.**

*For a wonderful alternative, add sliced grilled chicken or sautéed quail.*

# SANDERSON'S BLACK BEAN SALAD

1 (16-ounce) can black beans, drained
1 papaya (or mango), chopped
1 red pepper, chopped
1 jalapeño pepper, finely chopped
4 green onions, finely chopped
1 (10-ounce) box frozen corn, defrosted (or 1½ cups fresh corn)
¼ cup chopped fresh cilantro
¼ cup lemon juice
½ cup olive oil
Salt to taste

1. Combine first 6 ingredients and stir to blend.

2. Combine cilantro with lemon juice and slowly whisk in oil. Pour over beans and season to taste.

**Serves 8.**

*Great with Mexican dinner or backyard barbecue.*

# SOUTHWESTERN BLACK BEAN SALAD

**DRESSING**
¼ cup white wine vinegar
1½ teaspoons lime juice
1½ teaspoons Dijon mustard
1½ teaspoons chopped chives
½ teaspoon minced garlic
½ teaspoon ground cumin
Salt and pepper to taste
¾ cup olive oil

**SALAD**
1 (16-ounce) can black beans, drained
1 cup chopped onion
1 cup chopped bell pepper
1 cup corn
1 cup chopped celery
1 cup chopped tomato
¼ cup chopped cilantro

1. Combine dressing ingredients in order given, slowly whisking in oil until smooth.

2. Combine salad ingredients and toss with dressing.

**Serves 8-10.**

85

# WHITE BEAN SALAD

**SALAD**
1 pound white beans
1 (10-ounce) package frozen
corn
1 small red onion, chopped
(about ⅔ cup)
½ red bell pepper, chopped
(about ⅔ cup)
½ cup finely chopped basil

**DRESSING**
½ cup extra virgin olive oil
3 tablespoons balsamic
vinegar
3 tablespoons fresh lemon
juice
1 tablespoon minced garlic
1 teaspoon Tabasco sauce
Salt and pepper to taste

1. Soak beans overnight in cold water. Drain.

2. Simmer in 4 cups lightly salted water for about 1 hour until beans are tender, not mushy. Drain, place in large bowl, and cool.

3. Defrost frozen corn (or run package under hot water). Add corn and remaining salad ingredients to beans.

4. Whisk together dressing ingredients. Toss bean salad with dressing and season to taste.

**Serves 8-10.**

*Refrigerate covered up to 3 days.*

*Wonderful as vegetarian entrée with large salad and warm bread.*

# VERMICELLI SALAD

1 (12-ounce) package
vermicelli
1 (8-ounce) bottle Italian
salad dressing
1 teaspoon poppy seeds
1 teaspoon celery seed
½ teaspoon caraway seed
¼ teaspoon cayenne pepper
1 bunch green onions,
chopped
1 cup sliced celery
½ cup sweet pickle juice
Salt and garlic powder to taste

1. Cook vermicelli as directed on package.

2. Toss with remaining ingredients and marinate covered at least 12 hours in refrigerator.

**Serves 12 as side dish.**

# Pasta Harvest Salad

1 garlic clove
1 small bunch fresh basil
  (about ½ cup chopped)
½ cup Italian parsley
½ cup olive oil
1 (14-ounce) can artichoke
  hearts, rinsed and quartered
1 red onion, thinly sliced
1 pound fresh mushrooms,
  sliced
2 cups fresh broccoli florets,
  raw or blanched
24 cubes Feta cheese
1 pound spinach fettuccini,
  broken into bite-sized
  pieces

## GARNISH

12 cherry tomatoes
20 black olives
4 tablespoons pine nuts
Freshly ground black pepper
Parmesan cheese

1. Chop garlic, basil, and parsley in food processor. Add oil and process well.

2. Combine oil mixture with next 5 ingredients, mixing well in large serving bowl or shaking to mix well in 6-quart Tupperware container with lid.

3. Cook fettuccini according to package directions. Drain, place in serving dish, and allow to cool a few minutes. Toss well with vegetable mixture. Refrigerate until ready to serve.

4. To serve, garnish with tomatoes, olives, and pine nuts. Pass freshly ground pepper and Parmesan cheese.

**Serves 8.**

*Wonderful luncheon with fresh fruit salad and hot rolls.*

*Can substitute or add other vegetables.*

# PERFECT PASTA SALAD

6 whole chicken breasts
1 pound pasta (vermicelli,
 macaroni, or any favorite)
2 cups chopped bell peppers
1 cup chopped celery
12 green onions, chopped
3 hard boiled eggs, chopped
½ teaspoon crushed red
 peppers
¾ cup slivered almonds
1 (24-ounce) bottle ranch
 dressing
Salt and pepper to taste

1.  Preheat oven to 400°.
2.  Boil chicken breasts, skin, bone,
    and cut into bite-sized pieces.
    Reserve broth.
3.  Cook pasta in chicken broth
    until done.
4.  Bake almonds at 400° for 5
    minutes until browned.
5.  Combine all ingredients in large
    bowl or dish. Cover and chill in
    refrigerator before serving.

**Serves 20 (or more).**

*Best when prepared ahead.*

# RICE & ARTICHOKE SALAD

1 (7-ounce) package chicken-
 flavored rice vermicelli mix
2 (6-ounce) jars marinated
 artichoke hearts, drained
 and chopped
4 green onions, chopped
6 green olives, sliced
1 (4½-ounce) can sliced
 mushrooms
½ cup mayonnaise
¼ teaspoon curry powder
¼ cup dill pickle juice

1.  Cook rice according to direc-
    tions, then add artichokes,
    onions, olives, and mushrooms.
2.  Combine mayonnaise with curry
    powder and pickle juice. Add
    mixture to rice, blending well.
3.  Serve at room temperature.

**Serves 6-8.**

# COLD WILD RICE SALAD

1 (6¼-ounce) box Uncle Ben's Long Grain and Wild Rice
Olive oil for cooking
1 (4-ounce) can mushrooms, drained
⅓ cup slivered almonds
¼ cup chopped red onions
½ cup golden raisins
1 (8½-ounce) can peas, drained

1. Cook rice and let cool.
2. Add remaining ingredients, then refrigerate overnight.
3. Stir to fluff. Serve cold.

**Serves 10.**

# SUMMER BEEF SALAD

2 pounds rare leftover beef, sliced
2 avocados, thinly sliced
½ sweet red onion, thinly sliced

**MARINADE**
½ cup olive oil
½ cup wine vinegar
1½ teaspoons salt
¼ teaspoon pepper
Chopped fresh parsley

1. In 9" x 5" x 3" glass dish, layer beef, avocado, onion, in that order, twice.
2. Combine marinade ingredients and pour over layers. Marinate at least 1 hour.
3. Serve over crispy greens with hot bread.

**Serves 6.**

SOUPS, SALADS, & SANDWICHES

# FRENCH MARKET SANDWICHES

12 croissants
1 cup butter, room
    temperature
¼ cup prepared mustard
½ teaspoon poppy seeds
2 tablespoons minced onion
    or shallots
2 pounds ham, thinly sliced
12 slices Swiss cheese, cut to
    shape of croissant

1. Preheat oven to 325°.
2. Slice croissants in half horizontally.
3. Combine butter, mustard, poppy seeds, and onion. Spread on half of each croissant.
4. Top each with 2½-ounces ham and cheese slice.
5. Put halves together, wrap each sandwich in foil, and warm at 325° for 15 minutes.

**Serves 12.**

*Can freeze in foil and warm, unwrapped, at 325° for 25-30 minutes.*

# HAM BARBECUES

1 cup ketchup
½ cup brown sugar
⅓ cup water
2 tablespoons apple cider
    vinegar
¼ teaspoon nutmeg
¼ teaspoon dry mustard
1 pound cooked, chipped
    ham
6-8 buns

1. Preheat oven 325°.
2. Mix first 6 ingredients in 2-quart casserole dish.
3. Add small pieces of ham to the mixture, stirring until ham is covered.
4. Bake at 325° for 1 hour. Serve on buns.

**Serves 6.**

*Can keep warm in oven.*

# BIG WHEEL SANDWICH

1 8" round loaf sourdough
  bread
2 teaspoons prepared
  horseradish
¼ pound roast beef, thinly
  sliced
1 tablespoon mayonnaise
4 (1-ounce) slices Swiss
  cheese
2 tablespoons prepared
  mustard
¼ pound ham, thinly sliced
1 medium tomato, thinly
  sliced
4 slices bacon, cooked and
  drained
4 (1-ounce) slices American
  cheese
½ medium red onion, thinly
  sliced
¼ cup butter, softened
1 tablespoon toasted sesame
  seeds
½ teaspoon onion salt

1. Preheat oven to 400°.
2. Slice bread horizontally into 6
   equal layers.
3. Beginning with bottom slice of
   bread, layer ingredients as
   follows: bread slice, horseradish,
   roast beef; bread slice, mayonnaise, Swiss cheese; bread slice,
   mustard, ham; bread slice,
   tomato, bacon; bread slice,
   American cheese, onion. Top
   with final piece of bread.
4. Combine remaining ingredients
   and spread over top and sides of
   loaf.
5. Place loaf on baking sheet. Bake
   at 400° for 15-20 minutes or
   wrapped in foil at 250° for 1
   hour.
6. Slice into wedges and serve.

**Serves 8.**

# SPICY HAM SALAD

1 (6½-ounce) can chunk ham
2 boiled eggs
½ cup chopped pecans
Chopped green chilies
Chopped ripe olives
Sweet relish
Mayonnaise

1. Mix first 3 ingredients and
   remaining ingredients to taste.
2. Serve on lettuce or sandwich
   bread.

**Yields 2-2½ cups.**

*Alternative: Spread on crackers
for appetizer.*

# TEA ROOM CHICKEN SALAD

4 cups cooked and cubed
  chicken
2 cups unsweetened
  pineapple bits
2 cups walnut pieces
2 cups celery, cut in ½"
  pieces
2 tablespoons curry powder
1 tablespoon coarse black
  pepper
Salt to taste
Mayonnaise to hold together

1. Combine chicken with remaining ingredients, mixing well.

2. Refrigerate, then serve on croissants.

**Serves 6.**

# DEANNA'S CHICKEN SALAD

1 teaspoon vegetable oil
2 tablespoons soy sauce
2 tablespoons minced onion
1 teaspoon curry powder
4 whole chicken breasts,
  cooked, boned, and diced
½ cup sliced water chestnuts
½ cup chopped pecans
½ cup chopped seedless
  green grapes
½ cup chopped celery
2 teaspoons minced candied
  or ground ginger
1¼ cups mayonnaise
2 tablespoons wine vinegar

1. In small saucepan, briefly heat (1-2 minutes) oil, soy sauce, onion, and curry powder. Transfer to large mixing bowl.

2. Add remaining ingredients and mix well. Serve on rolls.

**Serves 6-8.**

*Depending on size of chicken breasts, add more pecans, grapes, and ginger to taste.*

ENTRÉES

# SOUTHWEST BEEF ENCHILADAS

2 tablespoons cornstarch
1 tablespoon water

**SAUCE**
2 (16-ounce) cans beef broth
3 tablespoons chili powder
¼ teaspoon garlic salt
½ teaspoon cumin
Salt and pepper to taste

**FILLING**
1 medium onion, chopped
1 garlic clove, minced
1 tablespoon vegetable oil
1 pound ground beef
1 (4½-ounce) can pitted ripe
   olives, chopped
½ cup sauce
2 cups shredded Cheddar and
   Monterey Jack cheeses,
   divided
12 corn tortillas

1. Preheat oven to 350°.

2. Combine cornstarch and water. In saucepan, combine sauce ingredients and bring to boil. Add cornstarch mixture and boil 1 minute. Lower heat and keep warm.

3. Sauté onion and garlic in oil until golden. Add meat and brown. Add olives, ½ cup sauce, and 1 cup cheeses, heating thoroughly.

4. Moisten tortillas in bowl of water and warm over low heat one at a time until soft.

5. Put strip of filling across each tortilla, roll up tightly, then place in 13" x 9"x 2" dish. Sprinkle with remaining cup of cheeses.

6. Bake at 350° for 10-15 minutes. Spoon remaining warm sauce over enchiladas and serve.

**Serves 4-6.**

***Entrées section note:*** *If recipe calls for Rotel tomatoes, you may substitute diced tomatoes and green chilies.*

# FIRECRACKER ENCHILADA CASSEROLE

2 pounds ground beef
1 large onion, chopped
2 tablespoons chili powder
2-3 teaspoons cumin
1 teaspoon salt
1 (15-ounce) can ranch-style beans
6 corn tortillas
1½ cups shredded Monterey Jack cheese
1½ cups shredded Cheddar cheese
1 (10-ounce) can Rotel tomatoes
1 (10¾-ounce) can cream of mushroom soup, undiluted

1. Preheat oven to 350°.
2. Cook ground beef and onion in large skillet until meat brown and onion tender. Drain.
3. Stir in chili powder, cumin, and salt. Cook meat mixture for 10 more minutes, adding water if necessary.
4. Spoon meat mixture into 13" x 9" x 2" baking dish. Layer beans, tortillas, and cheese over meat mixture.
5. Pour juice from tomatoes, then tomatoes, then soup over cheese.
6. Bake at 350° for 1 hour.

**Serves 8-10.**

# TACO CASSEROLE

1 pound ground beef (or turkey)
1 medium onion, chopped
1 (6-ounce) can tomato sauce
1 envelope taco seasoning mix
1 (16-ounce) can chili beans
1 (14½-ounce) can Rotel tomatoes
1 (9-ounce) bag Doritos chips
1 cup grated Cheddar and/or Monterey Jack cheese

1. Preheat oven to 375°.
2. Brown beef and onions. Drain grease.
3. Add all remaining ingredients except cheese and chips.
4. Crumble chips in bottom of 13" x 9" x 2" baking dish, pour beef mixture over chips, and top with grated cheese.
5. Bake at 375° for 20-30 minutes until bubbling hot.

**Serves 6-8.**

# TAMALE PIE

1 pound lean ground beef
1 cup chopped green pepper
1 cup chopped onion
1 (16-ounce) can tomato
sauce
½ cup sliced olives
1 tablespoon sugar
3 teaspoons chili powder
1 (12-ounce) can corn,
drained
1 garlic clove, minced
1 teaspoon salt
1 teaspoon pepper
6 ounces sharp Cheddar
cheese, grated
1 (8½-ounce) package corn
muffin mix

1. Preheat oven to 400°.
2. Sauté beef, green pepper, and onion.
3. Stir in tomato sauce and next 7 ingredients. Simmer 20-25 minutes until thickened.
4. Add cheese and stir until melted.
5. Pour mixture into 9" x 9" x 2" baking dish or 2-quart casserole.
6. Prepare corn muffin batter according to directions and pour over (do not stir into) meat mixture.
7. Bake at 400° for 20-25 minutes.

**Serves 4-6.**

# TEXAS RANCH CASSEROLE

2 pounds ground beef
1 medium onion, chopped
1 medium green bell pepper,
chopped (optional)
½ teaspoon salt
½ teaspoon pepper
2 (15-ounce) cans ranch style
beans or pinto beans
1 (15-ounce) can Spanish rice
1 (4-ounce) can chopped
green chilies
¼ pound Cheddar, Colby, or
Monterey Jack cheese,
grated

1. Preheat oven to 375°.
2. Brown meat partially. Add onion, green pepper, salt and pepper and continue to brown. Drain grease.
3. Add beans, rice, and chilies, and pour mixture into lightly greased 13" x 9" x 2" baking dish.
4. Top with cheese, cover, and cook at 375° for 30 minutes. Uncover and cook another 5-10 minutes until bubbling.

**Serves 8.**

# SAM BASS' CHILI

1 large onion, diced
1 medium green bell pepper,
diced
1 large celery stalk, diced
1 medium jalapeño pepper,
finely chopped
1 garlic clove, finely chopped
4 pounds lean ground beef
2 (4-ounce) cans chopped
green chilies
1 (15-ounce) can stewed
tomatoes
1 (6-ounce) can tomato paste
1 (3-ounce) bottle chili
powder
1 tablespoon cumin
6 ounces water
2 bay leaves
Hot pepper sauce to taste
Garlic salt to taste
Salt and pepper to taste
6 ounces beer (optional)

1. In large pot, sauté onion, green
   pepper, celery, jalapeño, and
   garlic. Add meat and brown.
2. Add remaining ingredients and
   consume other half of beer, if
   desired.
3. Cook 2-3 hours on low heat.

**Serves 8-10.**

*Cooked beans may be added just
before serving.*

# CHEESE MEAT LOAF

1 egg, slightly beaten
1 pound ground beef
3 slices bread, torn into small
pieces
1 tablespoon Worcestershire
sauce
¾ cup evaporated milk
5 ounces mozzarella cheese,
grated
Ketchup

1. Preheat oven to 350°.
2. Combine all ingredients except
   cheese and ketchup.
3. Place three-fourths of mixture
   into 9" x 5" x 3" loaf pan.
4. Cover with mozzarella cheese
   and add remaining meat mixture.
5. Cover with ketchup and bake at
   350° for 1½ hours.

**Serves 6.**

# MOORE MEAT LOAF, PLEASE!

2¼ pounds chopped meat (all beef; half beef and half turkey; or any combination of beef, pork, and veal)
1 teaspoon salt
1 teaspoon pepper
¼ cup chopped green onions or yellow onion
2 tablespoons chopped fresh parsley
½ teaspoon dried basil
⅓ cup dried bread crumbs
¼ cup chili sauce
1 teaspoon soy sauce
1 egg, lightly beaten
¼ cup milk
2-3 tablespoons ketchup or chili sauce

1. Preheat oven to 400°.
2. Mix all ingredients and spoon lightly into loaf pan or baking dish coated with vegetable spray. Do not pack too tightly.
3. Top with 2-3 tablespoons ketchup or chili sauce.
4. Bake at 400° for 15 minutes. Lower heat to 350° and bake for about 1 hour more.

**Serves 6.**

*In a hurry? Use muffin tins and reduce baking time to 30 minutes.*

*Good hot or cold. Freezes well.*

# MICROWAVED MEAT LOAF

1½ pounds ground meat
1 (8-ounce) jar spaghetti or marinara sauce
1-2 large eggs, beaten
¾ cup seasoned bread crumbs
2 tablespoons instant onion
2 tablespoons white Worcestershire sauce
2 tablespoons spicy mustard
1 teaspoon garlic salt
½ teaspoon pepper
½ cup grated Parmesan cheese, divided

1. Combine all ingredients except cheese in 1½-quart microwave-safe bowl or loaf pan.
2. Lightly pack down mixture and sprinkle with half of cheese.
3. Cook in microwave on high for 5 minutes. Rotate dish ½ turn and cook 5 minutes more.
4. Sprinkle with remaining cheese, rotate another ½ turn, and cook another 5 minutes.
5. Remove from microwave, cover with foil, and let stand 10 minutes before serving.

**Serves 6-8.**

# SWEET & SOUR MEATBALLS

## MEATBALLS

1 pound ground beef
1½ teaspoons salt
Pepper to taste
¾ cup oats
¾ cup milk
3 tablespoons finely chopped
  onion

## SAUCE

6 tablespoons finely chopped
  onion
2 tablespoons vinegar
½ cup water
2 tablespoons sugar
1 cup ketchup
2 tablespoons Worcestershire
  sauce

1. Preheat oven to 350°.
2. Combine all meatball ingredients, roll into balls, and place in 13″ x 9″ x 2″ baking dish.
3. Combine all sauce ingredients in saucepan, bring to boil, and pour over meatballs.
4. Bake at 350° for 45 minutes.

**Yields 12-15 meatballs.**

# OOH LA LA FRENCH STEW

2 pounds stew meat
1 onion, chopped
2 slices bread, cubed
3 potatoes, cubed
3 tablespoons sugar
1 (28-ounce) can whole
  tomatoes, cut
4 carrots, cut in pennies
3 tablespoons tapioca
1 tablespoon salt
1 teaspoon thyme
1 teaspoon oregano
½ cup red wine
1 (10-ounce) box frozen peas

1. Preheat oven to 250°.
2. In large roasting pan, combine all ingredients except wine and peas.
3. Cover and bake at 250° for 5 hours. Add wine and peas last half hour.

**Serves 6.**

# NORTH CAROLINA BRUNSWICK STEW

4 pounds chicken
2 pounds stew beef
1 (28-ounce) can tomatoes, chopped
4 medium onions, chopped
1 bunch celery, chopped
1 (1-pound) bag frozen white corn
1 (1-pound) bag frozen green peas
1 (1-pound) bag frozen lima beans

## SEASONING MIXTURE

1 cup butter
2 tablespoons salt
½ cup ketchup
¾ cup vinegar
¾ cup sugar
1 teaspoon pepper
1¼ teaspoons cayenne
1 tablespoon mustard

1. In large pot, cook chicken and stew beef together in about 3 quarts of water. (Can cook day ahead.)

2. Refrigerate stock until fat solidifies, then discard the fat.

3. Pick chicken off bones and return chicken and beef to pot with 6 cups of stock.

4. Add next 5 ingredients and cook for 4 hours on medium heat. Add lima beans last hour of cooking.

5. Add seasoning mixture and cook another hour. Thin with stock if needed.

**Serves 12-15.**

*Best if made a few days ahead so seasonings blend. Freezes well.*

# ME-MA'S GOULASH

2 tablespoons butter, melted
1 onion, chopped
1½ pounds ground round
   steak
Salt and pepper to taste
1 teaspoon celery seed
1 teaspoon chili powder
½ teaspoon garlic salt
½ teaspoon oregano
2 tablespoons Worcestershire
   sauce
1 (5-ounce) can spicy hot V-8
   juice
½ cup ketchup
1 (8-ounce) package small
   elbow macaroni
1 (14½-ounce) can chopped
   tomatoes, with juice

1. In large skillet, sauté onion in
   butter and brown beef.

2. Add seasonings, Worcestershire,
   V-8 juice, and ketchup.

3. Cook macaroni according to
   package directions.

4. Stir cooked macaroni and
   tomatoes with juice into beef
   mixture.

5. Cover and simmer 20-30 minutes.

**Serves 6.**

# AMY'S EASY BEEF TIPS

2 pounds chuck roast, cut in
   1" cubes
1 (10¾-ounce) can cream of
   mushroom soup
1 package dry onion soup mix
1 (12-ounce) can 7-Up

1. Preheat oven to 275°.

2. Put meat in 2-quart casserole
   dish. Spread mushroom soup
   over meat.

3. Sprinkle with dry soup mix and
   pour 7-Up over all. Do not
   season.

4. Bake at 275° for 4 hours and do
   not open oven door.

5. Remove from oven, stir, and let
   stand 30 minutes before serving.

6. Serve over rice, noodles, or
   potatoes.

**Serves 6-8.**

# BEEF BRISKET WITH BARBECUE SAUCE

1 3-4 pound beef brisket, trimmed
3 tablespoons liquid smoke
1/2 teaspoon celery salt
1/2 teaspoon onion salt
1 teaspoon garlic salt
3 tablespoons Worcestershire sauce
1/2 teaspoon black pepper
1 (6-ounce) bottle barbecue sauce

1. Place trimmed brisket in 13" x 9" x 2" baking dish.
2. Pour liquid smoke and salts over meat. Cover and marinate overnight.
3. When ready to cook, preheat oven to 275°.
4. Sprinkle brisket with Worcestershire and pepper. Cover and bake at 275° for 5 hours.
5. Remove from oven and drain. Pour barbecue sauce over brisket. Return to oven and bake uncovered for 1 hour more.

**Serves 8.**

# BRITT'S FAVORITE BEEF BRISKET

5-7 pound beef brisket, trimmed
**MARINADE**
2 (10 1/2-ounce) cans bouillon soup, undiluted
1 (4-ounce) bottle liquid smoke
1 (4-ounce) bottle soy sauce

1. Place brisket in roasting pan.
2. Mix marinade ingredients and pour over meat. Marinate overnight.
3. When ready to cook, preheat oven to 275°.
4. Cover brisket and bake at 275° for 6 hours.

**Serves 12.**

# AUNT NITA'S MARINATED FLANK STEAK

1 flank steak (about 2 pounds)
**MARINADE**
2 (6-ounce) cans pineapple
  juice
¼ cup light soy sauce
1 tablespoon brown sugar
1 teaspoon ground ginger

1.  Prick steak on both sides.
2.  Whisk marinade ingredients together and pour over meat. Refrigerate at least 4 hours or overnight.
3.  Grill about 5-10 minutes per side, depending on thickness and desired doneness.
4.  To serve, cut diagonally in slices.

**Serves 4-6.**

*Leftovers make great fajitas!*

# ESTHER'S LONDON BROIL

**MARINADE**
½ cup oil
¼ cup soy sauce
4 teaspoons Worcestershire
  sauce
2 tablespoons wine vinegar
2 teaspoons dry mustard
Chopped onion
1 teaspoon pepper
2 teaspoons fresh parsley
2 garlic cloves, minced

3-5 pounds London broil

1.  Combine marinade ingredients and mix well.
2.  Put meat in plastic bag and cover with marinade. Refrigerate 4 hours, turning bag frequently.
3.  Grill to desired doneness, then let rest 15 minutes. Slice thinly and serve.

**Serves 6-8.**

# MARINATED FILET MIGNON

## MARINADE
1 onion, sliced thin
2-3 large garlic cloves, minced
1-2 tablespoons black pepper
1-2 tablespoons dried thyme (¼ cup fresh)
¼ cup chopped fresh basil leaves
1 tablespoon Dijon mustard
2 tablespoons olive oil
⅓ cup dry red wine

1 (3-4 pound) beef tenderloin, fully trimmed
Salt and pepper to taste
Watercress or Italian parsley for garnish

1. Whisk marinade ingredients together and pour over meat.

2. Marinate beef at least 3 hours (up to 24 hours) in refrigerator, turning and basting several times.

3. When ready to cook, preheat oven to 400°.

4. Remove meat from marinade, place in roasting pan, and season with salt and pepper. Discard marinade.

5. Roast meat at 400° for 35 minutes, turning and basting in its own juices 2-3 times.

6. Test to see that meat is cooked rare. If needed, roast another 10 minutes.

7. Let stand for 15 minutes out of the oven before carving.

8. Garnish with watercress or Italian parsley.

**Serves 6-8.**

# ROAST LEG OF LAMB WITH SPICES

1 leg of lamb (5-6 pounds), trimmed
5 garlic cloves, cut in slivers
2 teaspoons freshly ground black pepper
2 teaspoons ground cumin
2 teaspoons paprika
1½ teaspoons ground coriander
½ teaspoon cayenne pepper
6 tablespoons olive oil
¼ cup fresh lemon juice
2 tablespoons minced garlic
½ cup chopped fresh cilantro
Mint sprigs for garnish

1. Make ½"-deep incisions in leg of lamb every 1"-2". Insert garlic sliver in each incision.

2. Combine remaining ingredients to make paste and rub over lamb.

3. Place lamb in roasting pan, cover, and let stand 3 hours in cool place or overnight in refrigerator.

4. Preheat oven to 350°. Roast lamb to desired doneness, basting a few times. For medium rare, roast about 1 hour and 10 minutes.

5. Garnish with mint sprigs.

**Serves 4-6.**

*Also delicious grilled with marinated eggplant and red onion.*

# LAMB-STUFFED EGGPLANT

1 large or 2 medium eggplant
1 cup rice
1 tablespoon olive oil
1 garlic clove, finely chopped
1 large onion, finely chopped
1 pound lean ground lamb
1 medium tomato, chopped
Juice of one lemon
2 teaspoons dried dill
1/4 cup chopped parsley
Salt and pepper to taste
4 tablespoons grated
    Parmesan cheese

1. Preheat oven to 375°.

2. Place 1" of water in 13" x 9" x 2" baking dish. Slice eggplant in half lengthwise and place face down in water. Microwave on HIGH for about 5 minutes until eggplant is tender.

3. Scoop out pulp and chop in food processor. Save eggplant shells to stuff.

4. Cook rice according to package directions.

5. Heat oil in 4-quart pot, add garlic and onion, and sauté about 5 minutes until wilted.

6. Add lamb, stirring and chopping with side of heavy metal spoon, until lamb is browned. Drain grease.

7. Add tomatoes, cover, and cook for 10 minutes.

8. Uncover and add eggplant pulp, lemon juice, dill, parsley, salt and pepper to taste. Mix in cooked rice.

9. Arrange eggplant shells in casserole dish and fill each with lamb and rice mixture. Top with cheese.

10. Bake at 375° for 30-40 minutes.

**Serves 4.**

# GIGI'S VEAL CASSEROLE

2 tablespoons butter
1 ½ pounds boneless veal, cubed

**SAUCE**

2 medium onions, sliced
¾ pound mushrooms, sliced
1 tablespoon minced fresh parsley
¼ cup white wine
¾ cup sour cream
½ teaspoon salt
½ teaspoon pepper

1. Preheat oven to 250°.

2. Dry and flour veal. In large skillet, melt butter and brown veal, then transfer to 13" x 9" x 2" baking dish.

3. Sauté onions and mushrooms in skillet until translucent. Remove from heat and stir in remaining ingredients.

4. Pour sauce over veal. Cover and bake at 250° for 1 hour until tender. Serve with noodles.

**Serves 6.**

# NUTRITIOUS & DELICIOUS VEAL CHOPS

2 (6-ounce) veal chops
½ teaspoon salt
Freshly ground black pepper (8 turns of pepper mill)
1 tablespoon olive oil
4 garlic cloves, minced
2 bay leaves
½ teaspoon dried thyme
¼ cup dry white wine
¼ cup chicken broth
1 cup peeled and diced ripe tomatoes

1. Sprinkle veal chops with salt and pepper.

2. In skillet, heat oil and brown veal chops on one side for 5 minutes.

3. Turn chops and add garlic, bay leaves, and thyme. Cook 5 minutes more.

4. Pour in wine, scraping and stirring to dissolve any solid particles clinging to pan.

5. Add chicken broth and tomatoes and bring to boil. Cover and simmer over low heat for 30 minutes.

6. Uncover and reduce sauce by half. Serve with pasta.

**Serves 2.**

# SWEET MUSTARD PORK CHOPS

1 cup dry bread crumbs
1 teaspoon seasoned salt
6 loin pork chops, trimmed
Sweet mustard

1. Preheat oven to 350° and spray 13" x 9" x 2" baking dish with no-stick cooking spray.

2. Combine bread crumbs and seasoned salt. Spread mustard on both sides of pork chop and dip into bread crumbs, coating both sides well.

3. Place chops in baking dish, cover, and bake at 350° for 45 minutes. Uncover and bake 15 minutes more.

**Serves 6.**

*Moist and delicious!!*

# VIENNESE PORK CHOPS WITH APPLES

4 center cut loin pork chops, 1" thick
2 teaspoons oil
3/4 teaspoon salt
Pinch of black pepper
2 Cortland or Rome apples, peeled and quartered
6 small white onions
1/8 cup seedless raisins
1/4 cup sweet sherry
1/4 cup water
1 1/2 tablespoons brown sugar
Pinch of thyme
1/8 teaspoon nutmeg

1. Preheat oven to 375°.

2. In skillet, heat oil and brown pork chops for 5 minutes on each side, then drain.

3. Sprinkle chops with salt and pepper and arrange in baking dish.

4. Cover chops with apples, onions, and raisins. Add remaining ingredients.

5. Cover and bake at 375° for 1 1/4 hours, uncovering for last 15 minutes to brown.

6. Check seasonings and add more if desired.

**Serves 4.**

# TEXAS INDONESIAN PORK

3 pounds pork loin, cubed to
1½" pieces
¾ teaspoon salt
Ground black pepper to taste
1 tablespoon ground
coriander
1 tablespoon ground cumin
⅛ cup oil
¼ cup sliced shallots
1 tablespoon brown sugar
4 tablespoons soy sauce
Dash of ground ginger
Juice of 3 limes

1. Combine pork and next 5 ingredients in large bowl. Stir well
and let stand 20 minutes.

2. Add remaining ingredients, mix
well, cover, and refrigerate at
least 4 hours, preferably overnight.

3. Broil pork in marinade 6" from
flame for 30-35 minutes. Baste
and turn meat twice.

4. Serve with rice and chutney.

**Serves 4-6.**

# HONEY-MUSTARD PORK TENDERLOIN

**MARINADE**

4 tablespoons honey
2 tablespoons cider vinegar
2 tablespoons brown sugar
1 tablespoon Dijon mustard
½ teaspoon paprika

1 (1-pound) pork tenderloin

1. Preheat oven to 375°.

2. In roasting pan, combine marinade ingredients thoroughly.
Add tenderloin and baste well
with sauce.

3. Roast at 375° for 20-30 minutes
until meat thermometer registers
160°, basting occasionally.

**Serves 4-6.**

# PORK TENDERLOIN WITH MUSTARD SAUCE

**MARINADE**
¼ cup soy sauce
¼ cup bourbon
2 tablespoons brown sugar

2½-3 pounds pork tenderloin

**MUSTARD SAUCE**
⅓ cup sour cream
⅓ cup mayonnaise
1 tablespoon dry mustard
1 tablespoon finely chopped
  green onions
1 teaspoon wine vinegar
Pepper to taste

1. Combine soy sauce, bourbon, and brown sugar.
2. Pour marinade over pork, cover, and refrigerate several hours or overnight.
3. Preheat oven to 300°.
4. Place meat on rack in shallow roasting pan. Bake at 300° for 1½ hours, basting several times with marinade.
5. Combine sauce ingredients. Slice meat and serve with sauce.

**Serves 4-5.**

*Good with sweet potatoes and applesauce.*

# SAUSAGE CASSEROLE

1 pound sausage
1 medium onion, chopped
¾ pound fresh mushrooms
2 tablespoons butter
1 (6¼-ounce) box Uncle
  Ben's Wild Rice
1 (10¾-ounce) can cream of
  mushroom soup
1 (8-ounce) carton sour cream
1 cup Cheddar cheese

1. Preheat oven to 350°.
2. Cook sausage and cut up. Sauté onions and mushrooms in butter.
3. Cook rice with seasonings as indicated on box.
4. Toss with soup and sour cream. Add sausage, onions, and mushrooms.
5. Pour into greased 13" x 9" x 2" baking dish. Top with Cheddar cheese and bake at 350° for 20-30 minutes.

**Serves 6-8.**

*May substitute 4-5 chicken breasts for sausage.*

# SAUSAGE SKILLET DINNER

1 pound pork sausage
1 medium onion, chopped
¼ teaspoon garlic powder
1 cup uncooked rice
3 cups hot water
2 chicken bouillon cubes
1 (10¾-ounce) can cream of
  mushroom soup
1 (15-ounce) can black-eyed
  peas, drained
1 (4½-ounce) can
  mushrooms, drained
Grated cheese (optional)

1. In large skillet, lightly brown sausage and onion. Drain.

2. Add next 4 ingredients, cover, and simmer 20-25 minutes.

3. Add soup, black-eyed peas, and mushrooms. Heat thoroughly.

4. Top with cheese last 5 minutes of cooking.

**Serves 6-8.**

*Can substitute green peas for black-eyed peas.*

# HARVEST CASSEROLE

2 tablespoons margarine
5 cups chopped green
  cabbage
1 medium onion, halved and
  sliced
1 cup sliced carrots
1 (15½-ounce) can red beans,
  drained (optional)
1 (8-ounce) can stewed
  tomatoes
1 tablespoon vinegar
⅓ cup grated Parmesan
  cheese
2 tablespoon flour
Dash of ground black pepper
1 pound reduced-fat smoked
  beef or turkey sausage

1. Preheat oven to 350°.

2. Melt margarine in Dutch oven over medium-high heat and sauté cabbage, onion, and carrots for about 5 minutes.

3. Add next 6 ingredients, stirring to mix well.

4. Spoon mixture into shallow, greased 2-quart casserole dish. Cut sausage into bite-sized pieces and arrange on top. Lightly pack down.

5. Cover and bake at 350° for 40 minutes until hot.

**Serves 8.**

# Polish Sausage & Cabbage

1 red cabbage (about 2 pounds), sliced
2 tablespoons butter
1/3 cup lemon juice
1/2 cup red wine or beef broth
1/2 teaspoon salt
1/2 teaspoon pepper
3/4 pound Polish sausage
2 teaspoons brown sugar
1 tablespoon cornstarch

1. Pour boiling water over cabbage in colander and drain well.
2. Melt butter in Dutch oven or large heavy skillet and add cabbage. Stir in lemon juice and cook about 5 minutes until cabbage is pink.
3. Add wine, salt, and pepper. Cover and simmer over medium-low heat for 45 minutes.
4. After 45 minutes, mix brown sugar and cornstarch and add to simmering ingredients. Bring to boil, stirring constantly.
5. Reduce heat, add sausage, cover, and cook 30 minutes more.

**Serves 4-6.**

# New Orleans Red Beans & Rice

3 quarts water
1 pound dry red kidney beans, rinsed
1 large onion, minced
2 garlic cloves, minced
1 tablespoon parsley
1 pound ham, cut in pieces, or sliced smoked sausage
2 bay leaves
Salt and pepper to taste

1. In 6-quart pot, boil water and add beans. Remove from heat and let soak 20-30 minutes.
2. Return beans to low heat and add onion, garlic, parsley, and more water if needed. Cover and cook for 1 hour.
3. Add meat and bay leaves. Cook covered for 1-2 hours more until beans are tender.
4. Season to taste and serve over rice.

**Serves 8.**

113

# JAMBALAYA

4 whole chicken breasts
2 (6-ounce) boxes Uncle Ben's Long Grain and Wild Rice
1 teaspoon olive oil
1 pound mild smoked sausage, sliced
1 pound hot smoke sausage, sliced
2 medium onions, finely chopped
1 medium bell pepper, finely chopped
1 pound ham, finely chopped
2 (6-ounce) cans tomato paste
1 teaspoon thyme
1/2 teaspoon basil
1/2 teaspoon coriander
1 1/2 teaspoons steak sauce
1 teaspoon bottled brown bouquet sauce
1 teaspoon Worcestershire sauce
Salt and pepper to taste

1. Boil chicken in 2 quarts water. After cooking, save water and chop chicken into bite-sized pieces.

2. Cook rice according to package directions, substituting the saved broth from the water.

3. In stock pot, heat oil and brown sausage over low heat. Drain off grease, leaving just enough to sauté onions and peppers.

4. Add onions and peppers. Sauté until soft. Add chicken and ham, stirring to mix well.

5. Add 1 can tomato paste and 2 cans water. Mix well. Add second can tomato paste and 2 more cans water. Mix well.

6. Gradually add seasonings and cooked rice. Cover and simmer until hot.

**Serves 8-10.**

# BAMBOO-SKEWERED CHICKEN

**MARINADE**
3 tablespoons dry white wine
¼ cup soy sauce
2 tablespoons lemon juice
2 tablespoons vegetable oil
1 garlic clove, minced
¾ teaspoon fines herbes
½ teaspoon ground ginger
½ teaspoon onion powder

2 pounds chicken, cut in 1″
cubes

1. Combine all marinade ingredients and add chicken. Marinate at least 3 hours in refrigerator.
2. Place chicken on bamboo or metal skewers. Grill 3-5 minutes on each side.

**Serves 4-5.**

# GRILLED HONEY MUSTARD CHICKEN

2½-3 pounds chicken, cut up
¼ cup white wine vinegar
6 tablespoons coarse Dijon
  mustard
3 tablespoons honey
½ cup olive oil
Salt and pepper to taste

1. Wash chicken and pat dry.
2. Combine vinegar, mustard, and honey in small bowl. Slowly add oil, whisking constantly until smooth. Season with salt and pepper.
3. Coat chicken with marinade. Cover and refrigerate several hours or overnight, turning the chicken occasionally.
4. Grill 30-45 minutes, basting regularly with marinade, until chicken is done.

**Serves 6.**

*Remove skin for delicious, low-fat meal.*

# ORANGE CHICKEN

2 (4-pound) chickens, cut up

**MARINADE**

1 cup fresh orange juice
3 tablespoons olive oil
4 garlic cloves, minced
3 tablespoons fresh rosemary
  leaves (or 1 tablespoon
  dried)
1 tablespoon fresh thyme (or
  1 teaspoon dried)
Salt and pepper to taste

1. Wash chickens, pat dry, and set aside.

2. In large bowl, whisk together marinade ingredients. Add chicken, turning to coat. Cover and refrigerate at least 3 hours or overnight, turning several times.

3. When ready to cook, heat broiler, place chicken and marinade in roasting pan, and broil chicken, bone side up, about 12 minutes.

4. Turn, baste, and broil chicken another 10-12 minutes. Drizzle with marinade.

**Serves 6-8.**

*Tarragon, basil, or marjoram may be substituted for rosemary.*

*If barbecuing, cover grill with foil to prevent marinade from burning and baste frequently.*

# LEMON GARLIC CHICKEN

6 lemons, halved and seeded
3 garlic cloves, minced
1 bunch Italian parsley, chopped
1 roasting chicken, butterflied
Lemon slices and parsley for garnish

1. Preheat oven to 325°.
2. In clay cooking dish or roasting pan, squeeze juice from lemons. Add squeezed lemon halves, garlic, and parsley.
3. Place chicken, breast side down, on marinade and marinate at least 3 hours or overnight in refrigerator.
4. Remove from refrigerator, turn chicken breast side up, and bake at 325° for 2½ hours in same dish with marinade.
5. Place chicken on serving dish, garnish with lemon slices and parsley.

**Serves 2-4.**

# NEWPORT CHICKEN

2 skinless and boneless whole large chicken breasts, cut in half
½ cup Italian bread crumbs
2 tablespoons olive oil
½ cup chutney
¼ teaspoon curry powder
1 garlic clove, minced
1 tablespoon finely chopped parsley
¼ cup sliced almonds
1 tablespoon margarine

1. Preheat oven to 350°.
2. Coat chicken with bread crumbs and place in well oiled 13" x 9" x 2" baking dish.
3. Combine chutney, curry, garlic, and parsley. Spread mixture over chicken.
4. Sprinkle with almonds and dot with margarine. Cover and bake at 350° for 1 hour.

**Serves 6.**

*Freeze leftovers.*

# CJ's Basil Chicken

1-2 tablespoons olive oil
1-2 tablespoons chopped
 fresh basil
1 teaspoon black pepper
½ teaspoon dry mustard
 (optional)
½ teaspoon celery flakes
 (optional)
Salt to taste
2-4 whole boneless, skinless
 chicken breasts
½ cup white wine

1. Heat olive oil in skillet on medium-high. Stir in basil, pepper, mustard, celery, and salt. Cook 1 minute.

2. Open chicken breasts flat and add to skillet. Turn as soon as meat turns white, about 5 minutes each side.

3. Add wine, reduce heat to low, and cover. Simmer 10-15 minutes.

**Serves 2-4.**

# Chicken Cacciatore

6-8 boneless chicken breasts,
 cut up
¼ cup olive oil
2 medium onions, cut in ¼"
 slices
2 garlic cloves, minced
1 (14-ounce) can tomatoes
1 (14-ounce) can tomato
 sauce
1 teaspoon salt
¼ teaspoon pepper
¼ teaspoon celery seed
1-2 bay leaves
1 teaspoon dried oregano or
 basil, crushed
¼ cup white wine

1. In skillet, brown chicken pieces in olive oil. Remove chicken and set aside.

2. Sauté onions and garlic until tender, then return chicken to skillet.

3. Add tomatoes, tomato sauce, and seasonings. Cover and simmer 30 minutes, stirring occasionally.

4. Stir in white wine and cook uncovered 15 minutes until tender. Serve over hot, buttered linguine.

**Serves 4-6.**

*Serve with Cheese Garlic Biscuits and Caesar Salad.*

# Healthy Meatballs

4 slices whole wheat bread
1½ cups skim milk
5 egg whites, lightly beaten
2-3 tablespoons onion flakes
1 tablespoon Worcestershire
 sauce (optional)
1 teaspoon garlic powder
¼ teaspoon black pepper
½ cup chopped fresh parsley
3 pounds ground turkey or
 chicken
Salt to taste

1. Preheat oven to 425°.
2. Soak bread in milk, add remaining ingredients, and mix well.
3. Shape in 2″ meatballs (about 35-40) and place on non-stick cookie sheet.
4. Bake at 425° for 30 minutes.

**Yields 35-40 meatballs.**

*Good over pasta with marinara sauce. May add Italian spices like oregano.*

# Fried-without-Frying Chicken

½ cup finely crushed corn
 flakes or bread crumbs
¼ teaspoon thyme
¼ teaspoon oregano
¼ teaspoon paprika
¼ teaspoon salt
8 skinned chicken legs and/or
 breasts
Egg white, skim milk, or
 nonfat yogurt for coating
Vegetable oil

1. Preheat oven to 350°.
2. Combine corn flakes or bread crumbs with seasonings.
3. Dip chicken legs in egg white, milk, or yogurt and dredge in crumbs to coat.
4. Place chicken legs on flat surface like cookie sheet or shallow casserole dish sprayed with non-stick cooking spray. Drizzle ½ teaspoon oil over each coated piece.
5. Bake at 350° for about 45 minutes. For the crispiness of real fried chicken, broil for last few minutes of cooking.

**Serves 4-6.**

119

# OVEN-FRIED SESAME CHICKEN

¾ cup all-purpose flour
3 tablespoons sesame seeds
1 teaspoon steak seasoning
4 boneless and skinless whole
 chicken breasts
3 tablespoons soy sauce
⅓ cup margarine, melted

1. Preheat oven to 400°.

2. Combine flour, sesame seeds, and steak seasoning.

3. Cut chicken into ¾" strips. Dip pieces into soy sauce and dredge in sesame seed mixture.

4. Place chicken in 13" x 9" x 2" baking dish, drizzle with margarine, and bake at 400° for 25 minutes.

**Serves 4-6.**

# KELLY'S HERB CHICKEN

¼ cup dried bread crumbs
1 tablespoon grated Parmesan
 cheese
½ teaspoon dried basil
½ teaspoon oregano
¼ teaspoon garlic salt
1 whole chicken breast,
 skinned and boned
¼ cup melted butter
¼ cup dry white wine
¼ cup chopped green onions
¼ cup dried parsley flakes

1. Preheat oven to 375°.

2. Combine first 5 ingredients, mixing well.

3. Dip chicken in melted butter, then dredge in bread crumb mixture. Save any remaining butter.

4. Place chicken in baking dish and cook at 375° for 30 minutes.

5. While chicken is cooking, combine wine, remaining butter, green onions, and parsley. Pour mixture over chicken and cook another 20 minutes.

**Serves 2.**

*Fabulous!*

# Spicy Peanut Chicken

3 cups onion, thinly sliced

5 skinless and boneless whole chicken breasts, cut in half

3 teaspoons ground cumin

1½ teaspoons ground cinnamon

## SAUCE

5 tablespoons canola or other vegetable oil

6 fresh plum tomatoes (or canned without juice)

1 jalapeño pepper (or ¼-½ teaspoon dried chili pepper)

3 tablespoons lemon juice

6 tablespoons peanut butter

3 large garlic cloves

1½ cups tomato puree

Cilantro leaves for garnish

1. Wash and dry chicken breasts. Rub with mixture of cumin and cinnamon.

2. Heat oil in large skillet and sauté onion until wilted. Add chicken to brown on both sides, about 5 minutes each side. Cook in batches, if needed.

3. Wash plum tomatoes and cut in large chunks.

4. Halve jalapeño pepper and remove seeds. Chop fine in food processor.

5. Add tomatoes, lemon juice, peanut butter, garlic, and tomato puree to food processor, blending well.

6. Pour sauce over chicken in skillet.

7. Cover, reduce heat, and simmer for 15-20 minutes until chicken is cooked.

8. Garnish with cilantro leaves and serve with brown basmati rice.

**Serves 8.**

*Avoid touching eyes when working with chilies. Wash hands well afterwards.*

# CHICKEN WELLINGTON

4 tablespoons butter

2 whole boneless, skinless chicken breasts, cut in half

Salt and freshly ground pepper to taste

8 ounces mushrooms, finely chopped

2 tablespoons flour

4 tablespoons whipping cream

2 tablespoons lemon juice

1 pre-rolled sheet frozen puff pastry

1 egg, beaten

1. Preheat oven to 400°.

2. Heat butter in heavy skillet and cook chicken breasts over moderate heat for about 7 minutes per side until cooked through. Remove chicken from skillet and season with salt and pepper. Cut into bite-sized pieces.

3. To skillet, add mushrooms and stir until soft. Sprinkle with flour and stir. Add cream, lemon juice, salt and pepper to taste. Continue to stir until mixture is smooth and thick. Set aside to cool.

4. On floured surface, roll out pastry sheet to measure 12" square and ⅛" thick. Cut pastry into four squares.

5. Place chicken pieces on each square and cover with mushroom mixture. Dampen edges of pastry and roll neatly around filling, tucking in ends.

6. Place seam side down on baking sheet and brush with beaten egg. Cut small slit in top for steam to escape, then bake at 400° for 25 minutes.

**Serves 4.**

# PENNSYLVANIA DUTCH CHICKEN POT PIE

1 (4-pound) chicken, cut up
12 cups water
1½ teaspoons salt (optional)
½ teaspoon pepper
1 celery stalk, diced
4 medium thin-skinned potatoes, peeled and quartered
1 large onion, coarsely chopped
4 large carrots, sliced in rounds
2 cups frozen green beans or peas
1 cup frozen corn (optional)
2 tablespoons parsley

## DUMPLINGS

2 cups flour
½ teaspoon salt
1 teaspoon baking powder
2 tablespoons vegetable shortening
1 egg, beaten
⅓ cup water

1. In 6-quart stock pot, simmer chicken in water with salt, pepper, and celery for 1 hour until tender. As chicken cooks, skim surface occasionally to remove fat.

2. Lift chicken from pot and remove skin and bones. Return meat to pot and add potatoes, onions, carrots, green beans, and corn.

3. Bring stock to boil and cook 15-20 minutes. Stir in parsley.

4. As chicken and vegetables boil, prepare dumplings. Combine flour, salt, and baking powder. Cut into shortening until mixture is cracker-meal fine.

5. Stir in egg and water, then roll out dough on lightly-floured board to ⅛" thick. Cut dough into 2" squares.

6. Drop squares into boiling chicken and vegetable broth. Cover and cook another 15-20 minutes until dumplings are tender.

7. Serve in wide bowls.

**Serves 12.**

*Hard but worth it for a very special family meal.*

# CHARLOTTE'S CHEESY CHICKEN

2 tablespoons margarine
3-4 whole boneless, skinless chicken breasts, cut in half
6-8 ounces mozzarella, Swiss, or Monterey Jack cheese
1 (10½-ounce) can cream of chicken soup
½ cup milk
2 cups garlic and onion croutons

1. Preheat oven to 375°.
2. Melt margarine in 13" x 9" x 2" baking dish.
3. Place breasts in margarine, coating each well, and cover with sliced or grated cheese.
4. Combine soup and milk and pour over chicken.
5. Sprinkle croutons on top and bake at 375° for 25-30 minutes. Serve over rice.

**Serves 6-8.**

# CHICKEN ARTICHOKE BAKE

4 whole chicken breasts, skinned and boned
1½ teaspoons salt
¼ teaspoon pepper
½ teaspoon paprika
6 tablespoons butter
¼ pound fresh mushrooms, cleaned and halved
1 (16-ounce) can artichoke hearts, drained

**SAUCE**

2 tablespoons flour
1 cup chicken broth
3 tablespoons sherry

1. Preheat oven to 375°.
2. Sprinkle chicken with salt, pepper, and paprika, then brown in 4 tablespoons butter.
3. After browning, place in 8" x 8" x 2" casserole dish.
4. With remaining 2 tablespoons butter, sauté mushrooms. Place on top of chicken and arrange artichokes around chicken.
5. Sprinkle flour in skillet, then add broth and sherry, stirring continuously. Cook 1 minute until thickened. Pour sauce over chicken and vegetables.
6. Cover and bake at 375° for 40 minutes. Serve over rice or noodles.

**Serves 4-6.**

# CHICKEN BREASTS & BROCCOLI

2 whole chicken breasts (4 halves)
2 large onions, quartered
6-8 celery stalks, quartered
2 (10-ounce) packages frozen broccoli spears
Juice of 1 lemon
2 (10¾-ounce) cans cream of chicken soup
1 cup mayonnaise
1 tablespoon curry powder
Salt and pepper to taste
½ cup grated Parmesan cheese
1 cup bread crumbs
Paprika for garnish

1. Preheat oven to 350°.

2. Boil chicken 45 minutes in 2-3 cups water seasoned with onion and celery. Drain and cut into bite-sized pieces.

3. Cook broccoli according to package directions.

4. Arrange chicken and broccoli in lightly buttered casserole dish. Squeeze lemon juice over all.

5. Combine soup, mayonnaise, curry powder, salt and pepper to taste. Pour over chicken and broccoli.

6. Top with Parmesan cheese and bread crumbs. Sprinkle with paprika.

7. Bake at 350° for 30 minutes.

**Serves 4.**

*Save chicken broth for soups and sauces.*

# KING RANCH MEXICAN CASSEROLE

1 (3-pound) chicken, boiled, boned, and cut into pieces
1 dozen corn tortillas, cut in small pieces
1 medium onion, chopped
2 cups grated Cheddar cheese
1 (10¾-ounce) can cream of mushroom soup
1 (10¾-ounce) can cream of chicken soup
½ (10-ounce) can Rotel tomatoes
½ cup chicken broth, reserved from boiling chicken

1. Preheat oven to 350°.
2. Prepare first 4 ingredients and set aside.
3. Combine last 4 ingredients.
4. In 13" x 9" x 2" greased casserole dish, layer ingredients as follows: half the chicken, tortillas, onion, cheese, and sauce. Repeat, switching the sauce and cheese to finish with cheese on top.
5. Bake at 350° for 45 minutes to 1 hour. Serve hot.

**Serves 6-8.**

# WHITE CHILI

1 medium onion, chopped
1 garlic clove, minced
1 teaspoon ground cumin
1 tablespoon canola or other vegetable oil
2 whole chicken breasts, skinless, boneless, cut into 1" chunks
1 (16-ounce) can cannellini beans (or Great Northern), drained
1 (16-ounce) can garbanzo beans, drained
1 can white corn, drained
2 (4-ounce) cans chopped green chilies
2 chicken bouillon cubes
Dash of Tabasco sauce
1½ cups water

1. Preheat oven to 350°.
2. Sauté onions, garlic, and cumin in oil.
3. In 2-quart casserole dish, combine sautéed mixture with remaining ingredients.
4. Cover and bake at 350° for 1 hour.

**Serves 6.**

# CHICKEN ENCHILADAS FLORENTINE

1½ pounds fresh or 2 packages frozen spinach
1 large white onion, finely chopped
3 tablespoons unsalted (sweet) butter
2 (4-ounce) cans chopped green chilies
3 cups sour cream
¼ cup milk
1 teaspoon ground cumin
¼ teaspoon garlic powder
¼ teaspoon salt
2 pounds boneless, skinless chicken breasts (3-4 whole breasts)
12 fajita-sized flour tortillas
8 ounces Monterey Jack and/or Cheddar cheese, grated

1. Preheat oven to 350° and lightly butter 15" x 10" x 2" baking dish.

2. Wash spinach and discard stems. Steam and drain, reserving ½ cup cooking liquid. Chop spinach coarsely and place in large mixing bowl with liquid.

3. In large skillet, sauté onion in butter, about 5 minutes until translucent.

4. Combine spinach, onion, chilies, sour cream, milk, cumin, garlic powder, and salt. Mix well.

5. In same skillet used for onions, poach chicken with water to cover, simmering about 20 minutes, until done. Cut into bite-sized pieces and set aside.

6. Soften tortillas in oven for about 3 minutes or microwave according to package directions (usually 45 seconds on high for whole package).

7. Add chicken to ½ of spinach mixture. Place equal amounts into tortillas and roll up. Place tortillas, seam side down, in baking dish in one layer.

8. Sprinkle tortillas with ½ of grated cheese, then cover with remaining spinach mixture. Top with remaining cheese.

9. Bake at 350° for 30-40 minutes until bubbling.

**Yields 12 enchiladas.**

# CORNISH HENS WITH PECAN STUFFING

½ stick butter
2 green onions, chopped
1 garlic clove, minced
1 cup Italian bread crumbs
½ cup grated Parmesan
  cheese
¼ cup chopped pecans
1 (6-ounce) can chopped
  mushrooms, drained
Dash of Tabasco sauce
¼ cup white wine
Salt and pepper to taste
2 Cornish hens

1. Preheat oven to 375°.
2. Melt butter in skillet and sauté onion and garlic.
3. Add bread crumbs and cheese, then add remaining ingredients except hens. Mix well, adding water if too dry.
4. Stuff mixture into hens, place hens in 9″ x 9″ x 2″ baking dish, and bake at 375° for 1 hour.

**Serves 2.**

# JACOS' MARINATED WILD DUCK

**DUCK MARINADE**
1½ cups vegetable oil
¾ cup soy sauce
½ cup Worcestershire sauce
2 tablespoons dry mustard
1 tablespoon black pepper
½ cup Burgundy wine
1½ teaspoons parsley flakes
2 garlic cloves, minced

3-4 wild duck breasts,
  cleaned and cut in half
1 bacon strip

1. Combine marinade ingredients.
2. Marinate duck breasts overnight. Remove breasts and discard marinade.
3. Wrap duck breasts with bacon strip and secure with toothpick.
4. Grill over hot coals for 30-40 minutes until breasts are cooked through. Serve with rice.

**Serves 6-8.**

*For wild duck, you can substitute domestic duck breasts, which are usually larger and more tender than wild duck so no need to marinate overnight.*

# EMMA MOREL ADLER'S MADEIRA SAUCE

1 pound fresh mushrooms,
   sliced
1 bunch green onions or 1
   onion, chopped
1 stick butter
2 tablespoons flour
2 cups chicken broth
7-8 ounces Madeira wine
1 tablespoon finely chopped
   fresh parsley (or 1 teaspoon
   dried)
Several green peppercorns in
   brine
Several crushed juniper
   berries (optional)
1-2 teaspoons red currant
   jelly (optional)
Salt to taste

1. Preheat oven to 375°.
2. Sauté mushrooms and green
   onions in half the butter.
3. In heavy frying pan, brown flour
   with remaining butter. Remove
   from heat and add chicken broth
   slowly, whisking to avoid lumps.
4. Return to heat and add sautéed
   mushrooms and onions. Add
   remaining ingredients.
5. Pour over broiled or sautéed
   chicken breasts or game bird.
   May add sauce to casserole of
   seared chicken breasts and bake
   at 375° for about 40 minutes
   until done.

**Yields sauce for at least 8
chicken breasts.**

*For typical Savannah dinner,
serve with wild rice and
creamed spinach.*

# AUNT ALICE STEINER'S CRABMEAT LAURA

## SAUCE

⅔ stick of butter
1½ tablespoons flour
1¼ cups milk
¼ cup chopped green onions
½ cup chopped fresh parsley
3 ounces Velveeta cheese, cubed
½ teaspoon horseradish
6-8 drops Tabasco sauce
Salt and cayenne pepper to taste

1 pound lump crabmeat
4 ramekins or pastry shells
Salt to taste
¼ cup dry vermouth

1. Preheat oven to 275°.

2. Make light roux: melt butter, add flour, and cook 10 minutes, stirring constantly. Add milk gradually.

3. Add onions and parsley and cook 10 more minutes, stirring constantly.

4. Add cheese and stir to make smooth sauce. Add horseradish, Tabasco, salt, and cayenne pepper.

5. Put crabmeat into individual ramekins or pastry shells, salt lightly, and season with vermouth.

6. Pour sauce over crabmeat and bake at 275° for 30-45 minutes until light brown and bubbly.

7. Serve with crusty French bread (for dipping!).

**Serves 4.**

# CRABMEAT AU GRATIN

**SAUCE**

2 celery stalks, chopped
1 cup chopped onions
1/4 pound margarine
1/3 cup all-purpose flour
1 (12-ounce) can evaporated
   milk
2 egg yolks
1 teaspoon salt
1/2 teaspoon red pepper

1 pound lump crabmeat
1/2 pound Cheddar cheese,
   grated and divided

1. Preheat oven to 375°.

2. Sauté celery and onions in margarine until clear. Add flour and blend until smooth. Slowly add evaporated milk, stirring constantly over medium heat.

3. Add egg yolks and mix well. Season with salt and pepper. Over low heat, warm mixture for 5 minutes, stirring constantly.

4. Place crabmeat in 2-quart casserole dish, then layer cheese, then sauce, then cheese.

5. Bake at 375° for 10-15 minutes until golden brown.

**Serves 4.**

# SUPREME CRABMEAT QUICHE

1 9" pie crust
1 cup lump crabmeat (or
   imitation crab)
3/4 cup grated Monterey Jack
   cheese
1 ounce imported capers
3 large eggs
1 1/2 cups heavy cream
1/4 teaspoon salt
3 tablespoons dry sherry

1. Preheat oven to 350°.

2. Layer bottom of pie crust with crab, cheese and capers.

3. Beat eggs with cream, salt, and sherry until smooth. Pour egg mixture over other ingredients and mix thoroughly.

4. Bake at 350° for 1 hour until puffed and brown.

**Serves 4-6.**

# SHRIMP CREOLE

1 medium onion, chopped
1 medium bell pepper, chopped
½ cup chopped celery
1 teaspoon minced garlic
2 tablespoons butter
1 (8-ounce) can tomato sauce
1 teaspoon flour
2 cups water
1 teaspoon Worcestershire sauce
Salt and pepper to taste
1 bay leaf
2 tablespoons chopped parsley
½ cup chopped green onions
2 pounds shrimp, shelled and deveined

1. Sauté onions, bell pepper, celery, and garlic in butter until tender, then add tomato sauce.
2. Dissolve flour in 3 tablespoons of water. Add flour mixture and remaining water to sauce.
3. Add remaining ingredients except shrimp and cook for 25-30 minutes on low heat.
4. Add shrimp and continue cooking another 10 minutes. Serve over rice.

**Serves 4-6.**

*Can substitute crawfish for shrimp.*

# SHRIMP PIE

3 cups fresh bread crumbs
3 cups milk, scalded
2 tablespoons butter, melted
2 tablespoons ketchup
1 tablespoon sherry
1 tablespoon grated onion
2 teaspoons Worcestershire sauce
½ teaspoon dry mustard
Dash of Tabasco sauce
Dash of cayenne
5 eggs, well beaten
1 pound shrimp, boiled, peeled, and deveined
Salt to taste
Bread crumbs and butter for topping

1. Preheat oven to 350°.
2. Soak bread crumbs in milk.
3. Add all other ingredients and mix thoroughly.
4. Put mixture into greased 13" x 9" x 2" baking dish. Sprinkle with bread crumbs, dot with butter, and bake at 350° for 30 minutes until firm.

**Serves 6-8.**

# SHRIMP MARGARITA

4 slices bread
1½ cups chopped onion
½ cup chopped bell pepper
½ cup chopped celery
½ stick margarine
1 pound shrimp, cleaned
1 (10-ounce) can Rotel
   tomatoes
1 (10¾-ounce) can cream of
   mushroom soup
2 cups cooked rice
½ cup parsley
½ cup green onion tops
Salt and pepper to taste
Bread crumbs and butter for
   topping

1. Preheat oven to 450°.

2. Soak bread in water; then squeeze water out, break into pieces, and set aside.

3. Sauté onions, peppers, and celery in margarine until clear. Add shrimp and tomatoes. Cook 5 minutes. Add remaining ingredients and bread pieces.

4. Pour into greased 13" x 9" x 2" baking dish, top with bread crumbs, and dot with butter. Bake at 450° for 30 minutes.

**Serves 6.**

*If preparing ahead of time, leave off bread crumbs and butter, then freeze. When ready to serve, thaw, add bread crumbs and butter, then bake.*

# SPICY BAKED SHRIMP

½ cup olive oil
2 tablespoons Cajun
   seasonings
2 tablespoons fresh lemon
   juice
2 tablespoons fresh parsley
1 tablespoon honey
1 tablespoon soy sauce
Pinch of cayenne pepper
1½ pounds uncooked large
   shrimp, shelled and
   deveined

1. Combine first 7 ingredients in 13" x 9" x 2" baking dish.

2. Add shrimp and toss to coat. Refrigerate for 1 hour.

3. Preheat oven to 450° and bake shrimp, stirring occasionally, about 10 minutes.

4. Garnish with lemon wedges and serve with rice or French bread.

**Serves 4.**

# MARINATED SWORDFISH WITH SALSA

2 tablespoons chopped fresh oregano (or 2 teaspoons dried)

2 tablespoons chopped fresh cilantro

3 tablespoons orange juice

2 tablespoons lime juice

1 garlic clove, minced

¼ teaspoon hot chili powder

4 (6-ounce) swordfish steaks

**SALSA**

8 ounces yellow, orange, or red bell pepper, diced

8 ounces yellow or cherry tomatoes, diced

8 ounces red tomato, diced

½ cup minced fresh basil

⅓ cup minced fresh parsley

8 olives (Greek, Italian, or French), pitted and sliced

1 tablespoon capers, rinsed and drained

1 tablespoon balsamic vinegar

1½ tablespoons lime juice

1. Combine first 6 ingredients and spoon mixture over swordfish in shallow bowl. Marinate at least 15-30 minutes.

2. Preheat broiler or prepare grill.

3. Prepare salsa by combining all ingredients.

4. Broil or grill swordfish steaks about 15-20 minutes. Baste several times on both sides.

5. Serve fish topped with salsa.

**Serves 4.**

*Also good with tuna, bluefish, or mackerel.*

*Rule of thumb: measure fish at its thickest point and cook 10 minutes to the inch.*

# GRILLED SWORDFISH WITH ORANGE ZINGER

6 ¾"-thick swordfish steaks
2 cups Italian salad dressing

**SAUCE**
3 sticks unsalted (sweet) butter
3 tablespoons white wine
3 tablespoons fresh orange juice
3 tablespoons grated orange peel
1 tablespoon lemon juice
1 tablespoon steak sauce
1 tablespoon Creole seasoning mix
4 small garlic cloves, minced

6 orange slices for garnish

1. Marinate swordfish in Italian salad dressing for 1-2 hours.
2. Combine sauce ingredients in heavy saucepan. Cook over medium heat until butter melts, then bring to boil until ingredients well blended, stirring frequently. Remove from heat.
3. Prepare barbecue grill.
4. Discard salad dressing. Grill swordfish steaks over high heat for about 8 minutes each side, basting with sauce.
5. Warm remaining sauce and pour over fish. Garnish with orange slices.

**Serves 6.**

# RED SNAPPER WITH ARTICHOKE HEARTS

2 tablespoons extra virgin olive oil
4 fillets fresh red snapper
½ cup dry white wine
½ cup diced red onion and extra for garnish
¼ cup drained capers
¼ cup marinated artichoke hearts with liquid
Freshly ground pepper to taste

1. Preheat oven to 200° and heat serving dish.
2. Heat oil in non-stick skillet and sauté fillets for 3 minutes each side. Remove fillets to heated dish, cover with foil, and place in oven.
3. Add wine, onion, and capers to skillet. Cover and sauté for 5 minutes. Add artichokes and sauté on high 2-3 minutes.
4. Pour sauce over fillets and sprinkle with onion.

**Serves 4.**

# BUTTER SAUCES FOR FISH

## BEURRE BLANC
## (WINE BUTTER SAUCE)

5 shallots, finely chopped
¼ cup vinegar
½ cup dry white wine
2 sticks unsalted (sweet)
  butter, room temperature
Salt, black pepper, and
  cayenne to taste
Fresh lemon juice

1.  Simmer shallots in vinegar and wine. Reduce until liquid almost evaporated, about 20 minutes.

2.  Cut butter into pieces and add to shallots, bit by bit, over very low heat so butter will not boil. Whisk continually until sauce is creamy and smooth.

3.  Season lightly with fresh salt, pepper, and pinch of cayenne. Add drops of fresh lemon juice to taste. Serve immediately over shell or fin fish.

    **Yields 1½ cups.**

## HERB BUTTER

½ cup unsalted (sweet) butter,
  softened
2 tablespoons chopped fresh
  parsley
1½ teaspoons minced fresh
  chives
1½ teaspoons minced fresh
  tarragon
1 teaspoon fresh lemon juice
Salt and pepper to taste

1.  Combine all ingredients and serve over favorite fish.

    **Yields ⅔ cup.**

# PASTA & VEGETARIAN DISHES

*Also see Hearty Soups, Main Dish Salads, and Entrées for recipes that can be made without meat, such as New Orleans Red Beans & Rice and Harvest Casserole.*

# ONE PAN CHICKEN SPAGHETTI

3-4 skinless and boneless whole chicken breasts, cut in half
5½ cups water, seasoned with salt, pepper, and garlic powder
2 celery stalks, finely chopped
2 medium onions, chopped
2 garlic cloves, crushed
1 (4-ounce) can sliced mushrooms
1 (16-ounce) can tomatoes, chopped
1 (10-ounce) package vermicelli, broken into pieces
½ (6-ounce) can sliced ripe olives
1 (10¾-ounce) can cream of mushroom soup
1 teaspoon Worcestershire sauce
2-3 dashes of paprika
Salt and pepper to taste
¾ pound Velveeta cheese, cubed

1. Simmer chicken in seasoned water about 30 minutes until done. Save 4 cups strained chicken broth.

2. Bone and cut chicken into bite-sized pieces. Set aside.

3. Add celery, onions, garlic, and mushrooms to strained chicken broth. Cook slowly for 10 minutes until tender, adding tomatoes for last 5 minutes.

4. Add spaghetti and cook 15 minutes until tender.

5. Add olives, soup, Worcestershire sauce, paprika, salt, and pepper. Stir well.

6. Add chicken and cheese, cook for about 2 minutes until cheese melts.

**Serves 6-8.**

*May be prepared ahead. Also freezes well after cooking. When ready to use, defrost and bake at 350° for about 45 minutes until bubbling.*

# STEVE'S CHICKEN SPAGHETTI SAUCE

2-3 pounds skinless, boneless chicken breasts
2-3 tablespoons olive oil
1 large onion, chopped
3-5 celery stalks, chopped
2 (6-ounce) cans tomato paste
3 (8-ounce) cans tomato sauce
2 (10-ounce) cans Rotel tomatoes, drained
1 garlic clove, minced
2 tablespoons sugar
2 tablespoons Italian seasoning
4 bay leaves

1. Simmer chicken in water until tender, then cut into bite-sized pieces. Reserve 1-2 cups chicken stock.

2. In 6-quart heavy pot, heat oil and sauté onion and celery until wilted.

3. Add next 7 ingredients. Simmer on low heat for 3-4 hours (longer the better), adding chicken stock as sauce thickens.

4. One hour before serving, add chicken pieces. Serve over favorite pasta.

**Yields about 6 cups.**

*For less spicy sauce, substitute 1 can regular tomatoes for Rotel tomatoes. Freezes well.*

# CAPELLINI WITH CRAB & VEGETABLES

4 ounces capellini (angel hair) pasta
2 tablespoons butter
½ pound fresh lump crabmeat
½ (7-ounce) can artichoke hearts, cut in quarters
½ (7-ounce) can palm hearts, cut in ½" circles
1 medium tomato, cut in eighths
⅓ cup freshly grated Parmesan cheese
Salt and pepper to taste

1. Cook pasta according to package directions.

2. Melt butter in non-stick skillet over medium-high heat and add remaining ingredients, stirring occasionally for 3-5 minutes until thoroughly heated.

3. Serve hot over pasta.

**Serves 2.**

# Uncle Ty's Clam Sauce

½ cup olive oil
3 tablespoons butter
4 garlic cloves, finely chopped
1 cup finely chopped onion
⅓ cup carrots, cut in matchsticks
½ cup white wine
3 (10-ounce) cans whole baby clams, with juice
3 small yellow or red tomatoes, halved and thinly sliced
1 tablespoon finely chopped basil
1 small bunch parsley, coarsely chopped
Salt and pepper to taste

1. Heat oil and butter in large skillet over medium heat, then sauté onions and garlic for 5 minutes.

2. Add carrots and sauté 5 more minutes.

3. Add wine and strained juice from clams and simmer 10-15 minutes, stirring often.

4. Add tomatoes, turn off heat, then add clams and remaining ingredients.

5. Stir and serve over hot linguini.

**Serves 4.**

# Puttanesca Pasta Sauce

4 garlic cloves
½ cup pitted black olives
4 teaspoons capers
¼ cup olive oil
2 (28-ounce) cans crushed tomatoes
2 (2-ounce) cans anchovies, drained
4 tablespoons chopped Italian parsley
1 teaspoon oregano

1. In food processor, finely chop garlic, olives, and capers.

2. In large skillet, heat oil and sauté olive mixture about 2 minutes until wilted, but not browned. Stir in tomatoes and simmer for 15 minutes.

3. Add chopped anchovies, parsley and oregano and cook 6-8 minutes more. Serve with penne pasta and Parmesan cheese.

**Yields about 6 cups.**

# PENNE WITH BROCCOFLOWER

1 head broccoflower (or broccoli), trimmed florets only
1 pound penne pasta
1/4 cup olive oil
2-3 garlic cloves, minced
3 anchovies, minced
Grated Parmesan cheese

1. Steam broccoflower and set aside.

2. Cook penne according to package directions.

3. While pasta is cooking, heat oil in large skillet and sauté garlic and anchovies for 30 seconds. Add broccoflower and cook 3-5 minutes.

4. Drain pasta and toss with broccoflower mixture. Serve with Parmesan cheese.

**Serves 4-6.**

# SHRIMP FETTUCINI

3 garlic cloves, minced
1/4 cup olive oil
1 cup sliced fresh mushrooms
1/2 cup sliced black olives (optional)
1/2 cup clam juice
1 tablespoon chopped fresh basil
1 tablespoon chopped fresh parsley
1 teaspoon dried oregano
1 pound fettuccini
1 pound large shrimp, shelled and deveined
3/4 cup cream
1 cup grated fontina cheese
Salt and pepper to taste

1. In large skillet, sauté garlic in oil until wilted. Add mushrooms and olives, simmer 10 minutes. Add clam juice, basil, parsley, and oregano. Simmer for 15-20 minutes.

2. While sauce is simmering, cook fettuccini in salted, boiling water to desired tenderness. Drain pasta and set aside.

3. Add shrimp to sauce and cook about 5 minutes until shrimp turns white. Add cream, cheese, salt, and pepper. Stir until cheese is melted.

4. Serve immediately over fettuccini.

**Serves 4.**

# SICILIAN PASTA WITH FRESH TUNA

4 tablespoons olive oil, divided
1 large onion, chopped
1 (35-ounce) can Italian tomatoes, chopped and juice reserved
1/2 teaspoon salt, divided
1/2 teaspoon pepper, divided
1 pound fresh tuna, cut in 1/2" pieces
1/4-1/2 cup chopped fresh mint (or basil)
3 garlic cloves, minced
1 pound linguini

1. Heat half the oil and sauté onion 10 minutes until soft. Add tomatoes and half the salt and pepper. Cook another 5 minutes until sauce slightly thickens. Remove and set aside.

2. Season tuna with remaining salt and pepper. Heat remaining oil in large skillet and sauté tuna about 4 minutes.

3. Add reserved tomato sauce, mint, and garlic. Cook 3-5 minutes more until tuna is medium-rare.

4. While cooking tuna, prepare linguini according to package.

5. Pour hot tuna sauce over pasta and serve immediately.

**Serves 4-6.**

# COUSIN PHIL'S CRAWFISH VERMICELLI

3 garlic cloves, finely chopped
2 tablespoons butter
4 tablespoons extra virgin olive oil
1 pound crawfish tails
1/2 pound mushrooms, sliced
3 tablespoons white wine
1 tablespoon Italian seasoning
Salt and pepper to taste
1 (16-ounce) package vermicelli
1/2 cup grated Parmesan or Romano cheese
1/4 cup parsley flakes

1. Sauté garlic in butter and oil.

2. Add crawfish tails, mushrooms, wine, and seasonings. Cover and simmer 10-15 minutes.

3. While sauce is simmering, cook pasta according to package.

4. Combine cheese with parsley.

5. In serving bowl, top pasta with crawfish sauce, sprinkle with cheese mixture, and serve.

**Serves 4.**

# FETTUCINI PRIMAVERA À LA ANN

¼ cup butter
1 onion, finely chopped
2 garlic cloves, minced
½ cup grated Parmesan cheese
1 cup sour cream
½ pound bacon
1 pound snow peas, stems and ends removed
1 red pepper, halved and seeded
1 yellow pepper, halved and seeded
1 pound fettuccini

1. Preheat oven to 350°.
2. In large skillet, melt butter, then sauté onion and garlic until wilted. Stir in cheese and sour cream. Remove from heat.
3. Microwave bacon and chop fine. Add to sauce.
4. Blanch snow peas for 30 seconds in boiling water. Rinse in cold water, then add to sauce.
5. Chop peppers into ¼″ squares and add to sauce.
6. Cook fettuccini al dente. Drain. Toss pasta with sauce and place in 13″ x 9″ x 2″ baking dish.
7. Bake at 350° for 10-15 minutes and stir before serving.

**Serves 4 as main course.**

# SAUSAGE ZITI BAKE

1½ pounds sweet Italian sausage, cut in ½″ slices
1 (32-ounce) jar favorite spaghetti sauce
1 medium onion, chopped
2½ cups sliced fresh mushrooms
Salt and pepper to taste
1 (16-ounce) package ziti
1 cup grated mozzarella cheese

1. Preheat oven to 350°.
2. Brown sausage. Add next 4 ingredients. Simmer 5 minutes.
3. Cook ziti al dente and drain. Combine with sauce in 13″ x 9″ x 2″ baking dish and top with cheese.
4. Cover and bake at 350° for 20 minutes, then uncover and bake 10 minutes more.

**Serves 4-6.**

# SPINACH LASAGNA

1 pound Italian sausage
(optional)

## SPINACH MIXTURE

1 medium onion, chopped
2 garlic cloves, minced
1 tablespoon olive oil
2 cups chopped fresh spinach
1 pound cottage cheese (1%
or 2%)
2 egg whites, beaten
1/4 teaspoon pepper
2 teaspoons parsley
1/2 cup grated Parmesan
cheese

## TOMATO SAUCE

2 (14-ounce) cans tomato
puree
2-3 tablespoons fresh basil (or
1-2 teaspoons dried)
1/2-1 teaspoon dried oregano

1 (1-pound) box whole wheat
lasagna noodles
1 pound mozzarella cheese,
grated

1. Preheat oven to 350°.
2. Cook Italian sausage and slice.
3. Sauté onion and garlic in olive oil for about 5 minutes until translucent. Transfer to large mixing bowl and add next 6 ingredients. Set spinach mixture aside.
4. Mix tomato puree with basil and oregano. Set tomato sauce aside.
5. Cook lasagna noodles in salted, boiling water until slightly firm and drain.
6. In 13" x 9" x 2" baking dish, layer twice as follows: noodles, spinach mixture, sausage (if desired), tomato sauce, and mozzarella cheese.
7. Bake at 350° for about 45 minutes until bubbling and slightly brown. Let stand 5-10 minutes before cutting.

**Serves 4-6.**

# PASTA WITH EGGPLANT

2 pounds eggplant, unpeeled
½ cup olive oil
2 garlic cloves, chopped
Salt and pepper to taste

**SAUCE**

1 medium red onion, finely
  chopped
2 tablespoons olive oil
1½ pounds ripe plum
  tomatoes (or canned)
Salt and pepper to taste
½ cup chopped fresh basil

1 pound rigatoni or penne
¼ pound Parmesan cheese,
  grated

1. Wash eggplants well and slice into ¼" discs. In large bowl, brush both sides of eggplant with about ⅓ cup of olive oil and sprinkle with chopped garlic, salt and pepper to taste. Let rest for 5 minutes.

2. Preheat broiler and broil eggplant slices about 5-10 minutes each side, watching carefully to make sure they do not burn. Return eggplant to bowl, drizzle with remaining olive oil, and set aside.

3. Prepare sauce: Sauté onion in oil for about 5 minutes. Add chopped tomatoes and simmer for 25 minutes, seasoning with salt and pepper to taste. Add basil during last 5 minutes.

4. While sauce is simmering, cook pasta according to package directions, usually about 10-12 minutes in salted, boiling water.

5. Drain pasta, toss with sauce, and add eggplant. Serve with Parmesan cheese.

**Serves 4-6.**

*Sauce can be made ahead and frozen.*

# PASTA WITH PESTO (BASIL) SAUCE

2 cups tightly packed fresh
  basil leaves
1/4 cup chopped Italian parsley
2 garlic cloves
1/2 cup pine (pignoli) nuts
1/2 cup freshly grated
  Parmesan cheese
1/2 teaspoon salt
1/2-3/4 cup extra virgin olive oil

1. In food processor, mince basil, parsley, and garlic. Add pine nuts, cheese, and salt.

2. Add olive oil through feed tube, processing about 5 seconds, until smooth paste forms.

3. Cook favorite pasta and toss with 1/2 cup pesto or less for each pound of pasta.

**Yields about 2 cups.**

*Also great on cold chicken and broccoli salads.*

*Leftover pesto may be frozen or stored. If storing, spoon in glass or plastic container, cover with about 1/2" of olive oil, cover tightly, and store in refrigerator.*

# PASTA WITH SUN-DRIED TOMATOES

1 pound fusilli
4 garlic cloves, 2 minced,
  2 sliced
1/4 cup olive oil
1 (10-ounce) box frozen peas,
  defrosted
1/3 pound sun-dried tomatoes
  in oil, sliced into strips
Salt to taste
2 tablespoons chopped fresh
  basil (optional)
1/4 pound Parmesan cheese,
  grated

1. Cook pasta al dente and drain.

2. In large skillet, sauté garlic in oil about 5 minutes. Gradually add pasta, turning to coat in oil.

3. Add peas and tomatoes, along with their oil. Cook over medium heat until mixture is warm, without letting peas lose their bright color.

4. Add salt to taste and serve with fresh basil and Parmesan cheese.

**Serves 2-4 as main dish.**

# JEANNE'S PENNE WITH TOMATOES & BASIL

3-4 medium-sized fresh
  tomatoes
3 garlic cloves, minced
¼ cup chopped fresh basil
Salt to taste
1 pound penne pasta
¼ cup extra virgin olive oil
¼ cup freshly grated
  Parmesan cheese

1.  Peel and seed tomatoes. To peel, cut "X" in bottom of each tomato, drop in boiling water for 30 seconds until skin loosens, then peel. To seed, cut crosswise and squeeze out seeds.

2.  Dice tomatoes and mix with garlic, basil and salt.

3.  Cook penne according to package. Drain and place in warm serving bowl.

4.  Toss with oil, then add tomato and basil mixture. Serve with Parmesan cheese.

**Serves 6.**

*No substitutes for fresh tomatoes and basil!*

# PENNE RESTUCCIA

1 pound brie cheese
3-4 medium fresh tomatoes
3 garlic cloves, minced
1 cup chopped fresh basil
Salt to taste
1 pound penne pasta

1.  Remove skin of brie, cut in cubes, and set aside.

2.  Peel, seed, and dice tomatoes. (See first direction in recipe above.)

3.  Place tomatoes in bowl and mix with garlic, basil, brie, and salt. Let marinate at room temperature 2 hours.

4.  When ready to serve, cook penne according to package. Drain and toss with brie mixture.

**Serves 6.**

# VEGETARIAN'S DELIGHT

1 large uncooked potato, peeled and cut in ½" cubes

1 medium green pepper, cut into thin strips

2 zucchini, thinly sliced

2 medium onions, chopped

2 carrots, sliced

2 tablespoons chopped parsley

1 (10-ounce) package frozen green peas

¾ cup uncooked white or brown rice

1 (1 pound, 12-ounce) can tomatoes, chopped with juice

⅓ cup and 3 tablespoons olive oil

2 tablespoons tarragon vinegar (or lemon juice)

3 teaspoons salt

1 teaspoon pepper

Dash of Tabasco sauce

1 cup grated Monterey Jack cheese

1. Preheat oven to 350°.

2. Layer vegetables and rice (first 8 ingredients) in 13" x 9" x 2" casserole dish.

3. Combine tomatoes with juice, oil, vinegar, salt, pepper, and Tabasco sauce and pour over vegetables.

4. Cover casserole and bake at 350° for 1½ hours. During last 10 minutes, uncover and sprinkle with grated cheese. Bake until cheese is melted.

**Serves 8-10.**

*Serve with salad and bread for a delicious meatless meal.*

*May freeze after baking.*

# Spicy Vegetarian Chili

2 tablespoons vegetable oil
2 large onions, chopped
4 large garlic cloves, finely chopped
1-2 jalapeño chilies, minced
2 (28-ounce) can Italian plum tomatoes, diced and juice reserved
½ cup tomato paste
2 bell peppers, chopped
2 large carrots, chopped
1 tablespoon ground cumin
¾ teaspoon salt
½ teaspoon cayenne pepper
2 (15-ounce) cans kidney beans, drained
2 (15-ounce) cans pinto beans, drained
2 small zucchini, diced
Grated Cheddar cheese
Chopped onions

1.  Heat oil in heavy, large pot over medium heat. Sauté onions, garlic, and chilies about 5 minutes until onions are translucent.

2.  Add tomatoes, 1 cup reserved tomato juice, and next 6 ingredients. Simmer 20 minutes, stirring frequently.

3.  Add beans and cook another 15 minutes, thinning with reserved tomato juice if needed.

4.  Add zucchini and cook another 5 minutes.

5.  Ladle chili into bowls and pass the cheese and onions. Serve with hot cornbread for a complete meal.

**Yields 12 cups.**

# Pinto Beans

1 pound dried pinto beans
Chicken or vegetable stock
1 tablespoon chili powder
1 tablespoon sugar
1 tablespoon salt
2 tablespoons cumin
1 tablespoon pepper
½ cup chopped onion
½ stick butter
2 ham hocks (optional)

1.  Wash and sort beans. In large bowl, place 1 part beans to 2 parts water. Soak beans overnight.

3.  Next morning, pour off water and transfer beans to stock pot. Cover 1 part beans with 2 parts chicken or vegetable stock.

4.  Add remaining ingredients and simmer 3 hours, stirring occasionally.

5.  Serve hot with cornbread.

**Serves 6.**

# EL RANCHO GRANDE

1 cup cornmeal
1 teaspoon salt
½ teaspoon baking soda
1 cup milk
2 eggs, beaten
¼ cup vegetable oil
2 cups cooked rice
1 (16½-ounce) can cream-
   style corn
½ cup finely chopped onion
1 teaspoon dried hot peppers
   (optional)
½ pound Cheddar cheese,
   grated

1. Preheat oven to 350°.
2. Sift dry ingredients together in large mixing bowl. Add remaining ingredients, stirring only to blend.
3. Pour into 12" oven-proof skillet or greased 13" x 9" x 2" casserole dish sprinkled with cornmeal. Bake at 350° for 50 minutes until golden brown.

**Serves 8-10.**

*Serve piping hot as entrée with beans and salad or as side dish.*

# TEX-MEX FRITTATA

1 tablespoon butter
5-6 large eggs
⅔ cup grated mild Cheddar
   cheese
⅓ cup red or green salsa
½ cup coarsely chopped
   tomatoes
3 tablespoons chopped green
   chilies
3 tablespoons chopped black
   olives
Salt and pepper to taste

1. Heat butter in medium-large skillet. Beat eggs and cheese together. Add to skillet and cook over medium heat, stirring lightly until bottom begins to set.
2. As eggs become firm, add remaining ingredients, spreading evenly over top.
3. Cook 5-7 minutes until frittata is golden brown on bottom and set on top.
4. Loosen edges and slide onto serving plate. Cut into wedges and serve with salad and bread.

**Serves 4.**

*For variety, add avocado slices or diced artichoke hearts.*

# BLACK-EYED PEAS & KALE RAGOUT

1 pound dry black-eyed peas
6 cups cold water
1 teaspoon salt
1 jalapeño pepper, seeded
and coarsely chopped
(optional)
8 ounces Virginia ham,
pancetta, or bacon, cut into
3/4" pieces (optional)
2 medium onions, chopped
4 garlic cloves, minced
1½ pounds kale, collard
greens or spinach, leaves
cut into 2" pieces and stems
into ½" pieces
Hot pepper sauce (optional)

1. Wash peas and discard any damaged ones. Place in pot with cold water, salt, and jalapeño pepper. Bring to boil, reduce heat, and cover. Simmer for 45 minutes until tender.

2. While peas are cooking, cook ham pieces in saucepan over medium heat about 10 minutes until browned. Add onions and garlic and sauté about 2 minutes.

3. Wash kale carefully under cool water and add to ham in saucepan. Press down on kale to contain in pan, cover, and cook until wilted.

4. Combine kale mixture with beans, stir, bring to boil, then simmer together for about 10 minutes.

5. Add hot pepper sauce, if desired, and serve with brown rice.

**Serves 6.**

*Omit ham for complete vegetarian meal.*

# SPINACH PIE PARMA

2 cups seasoned croutons
¼ cup butter, melted
1 (10-ounce) package frozen chopped spinach, thawed and drained
1 cup cottage cheese
4 ounces Monterey Jack cheese
3 eggs, beaten
¼ cup chopped onion
3 tablespoons sour cream
Garlic salt to taste
¼ cup grated Parmesan cheese for topping

1.  Preheat oven to 350°.
2.  Crush croutons, combine with butter, and press into 9" pie pan.
3.  Combine spinach with next 6 ingredients. Mix well and spoon over crust.
4.  Bake at 350° for 30 minutes until set. Remove from oven, sprinkle with Parmesan cheese and let stand for 10 minutes before serving.

**Serves 8-10.**

# WHITE GARLIC PIZZA

Dough for ready-made pizza crust
4 tablespoons margarine
4-5 garlic cloves, minced
½ pound shredded mozzarella
Dash of oregano

1.  Preheat oven to 425°.
2.  Grease pizza pan or cookie sheet and pat dough into pan.
3.  Melt margarine and sauté garlic over medium heat for about 5 minutes until golden and soft, but not brown.
4.  Spread margarine and garlic over prepared dough, leaving ½" edge around pizza. Sprinkle with cheese and oregano.
5.  Bake at 425° about 15-20 minutes until cheese is lightly browned and crust is crispy.

**Yields 8 pieces.**

*Before adding cheese and spices, may add 2 cups parboiled, chopped vegetable.*

# VEGETABLES & SIDE DISHES

## Vegetables

## Potatoes

## Rice

## Other

# HERBED BROCCOLI

1½ pounds fresh broccoli
2 chicken flavored bouillon
cubes
1 cup water
¼ cup chopped onion
(optional)
1 teaspoon dried marjoram
1 teaspoon dried basil
3 tablespoons butter or
margarine, melted

1. Cut broccoli into spears and wash thoroughly. Set aside.

2. Combine bouillon cubes and water in large skillet, cooking over medium heat until bouillon dissolves.

3. Stir in onion, marjoram, and basil. Add broccoli, cover, reduce heat, and simmer 10 minutes until tender.

4. Drain and arrange on platter. Drizzle with butter and serve.

**Serves 6.**

# ESCALLOPED CORN

1 stick margarine
1 (7-ounce) can creamed corn
1 (7-ounce) can whole kernel
corn, drained
1 (8-ounce) container sour
cream
2 eggs
1 (8½-ounce) box cornbread
mix
4 ounces shredded Monterey
Jack cheese (optional)
½ (4-ounce) can chopped
green chilies (optional)

1. Preheat oven to 350°.

2. Melt margarine and add both cans of corn. Stir in sour cream.

3. Beat eggs and fold into corn mixture. Stir in cornbread mix and add remaining ingredients, if desired.

4. Pour into lightly greased 13" x 9" x 2" glass dish and bake at 350° for 1 hour.

**Serves 6-8.**

# CREOLE EGGPLANT

3 eggplants, peeled and sliced
3 medium onions, peeled and sliced
6 tomatoes, peeled and sliced
3 green peppers, sliced into rings
Salt and pepper to taste
Grated Parmesan cheese to taste
6 tablespoons melted butter or margarine

1. Preheat oven to 350°.
2. Layer vegetables in lightly greased 13" x 9" x 2" casserole dish, seasoning each layer with salt and pepper.
3. Sprinkle with Parmesan cheese and cover with butter.
4. Cover and bake 45 minutes, then uncover and bake another 10 minutes.

**Serves 16.**

# GLAZED CARROTS & ONIONS

4 carrots, peeled and sliced
12 small pearl onions, peeled
1½ cups chicken broth
4 tablespoons butter
2 tablespoons sugar
Salt and pepper to taste

1. Heat chicken broth and butter in saucepan. Add sugar, carrots, and onions. Salt and pepper to taste.
2. Cover and cook until liquid turns into glaze, about 20 minutes.

**Serves 4.**

# "O' ONIONS"

4 medium onions, quartered
2 tablespoons balsamic vinegar
1 tablespoon olive oil
1 teaspoon Jane's Krazy Mixed-Up Pepper (or salt and pepper to taste)

1. Preheat oven to 350°.
2. Place quartered onions in zip-lock bag. Pour in vinegar, oil, and pepper.
3. Shake, remove from bag and bake at 350° for 45 minutes.

**Serves 4.**

*Also good baked with roast.*

# Margaret's Squash Casserole

2-3 pounds yellow squash, sliced
12 saltine crackers, crumbled
¼ cup grated onion
¼ cup milk
1 egg, beaten
Freshly ground black pepper to taste
1 cup grated Cheddar cheese

1. Preheat oven to 350°.
2. Boil or steam squash in water, drain, and mash.
3. Add crumbled crackers and onion to squash.
4. Whisk milk and egg together. Add to squash and season to taste.
5. Pour into 11" x 7" x 2" casserole dish and cover with cheese. Bake at 350° for 30-40 minutes.

**Serves 6-8.**

*May be frozen and baked at later date. Fast, easy, and sure winner!*

# Mexican Yellow Squash Casserole

2-3 pounds yellow squash, sliced
½ cup chopped onion
1 tablespoon butter or margarine
1 cup crushed corn chips
1 cup grated Cheddar cheese
1 egg, beaten
¼ cup chopped green onions tops
2 tablespoons jalapeño peppers (or to taste)
Salt and pepper to taste

1. Preheat oven to 350°.
2. Cook squash in small amount of boiled, salted water until just tender. Drain and mash well.
3. Sauté onion in butter. In large bowl, combine squash and onion.
4. Stir in remaining ingredients and pour into 11" x 7" x 2" casserole dish. Bake at 350° for 30-40 minutes.

**Serves 6.**

# Southern-Style Squash Casserole

1 cup whole milk
1 cup soft whole wheat bread crumbs
2 cups chopped cooked yellow or zucchini squash
1 egg, beaten
1½ cups grated sharp Cheddar cheese
2½ tablespoons chopped parsley
½ (4-ounce) jar chopped pimentos
2 tablespoons chopped onions
1 tablespoon butter or margarine, melted
Dash of black pepper

1. Preheat oven to 350°.
2. Scald milk and add bread crumbs.
3. Stir in squash, egg, and cheese.
4. Mix in remaining ingredients and place in greased 2-quart casserole dish. Bake at 350° for 1 hour.

**Serves 6.**

*Wonderful with turkey and ham!*

# Roasted Vegetables

Any vegetables: broccoli, cauliflower, squash, carrots, onions, tomatoes, potatoes, etc.
Olive oil
Garlic cloves, chopped
Salt

1. Preheat oven to 475°.
2. Wash, trim and cut up vegetables. Parboil or steam carrots and potatoes for a few minutes; drain.
3. Toss vegetables with olive oil, garlic, and salt.
4. Place in roasting pan in one layer and roast at 475° until cooked to desired doneness. Serve hot or room temperature.

**Serves 6.**

*Try adding fresh herbs like basil and grilling.*

# Spaghetti Squash

1 spaghetti squash
1 cup grated Fontina cheese
  (or other favorite cheese)
2 tablespoons margarine
Salt and pepper to taste

1.  Preheat oven to 350°.
2.  With fork, punch holes all around squash and place on cookie sheet. Bake at 350° for 1½ hours, turning after 45 minutes.
3.  Cut off top quarter of squash, remove pulp and seeds, and scrape out squash, including top.
4.  In bowl, mix squash with remaining ingredients.
5.  Place mixture in lightly greased casserole dish or back into shell of squash and bake about 15 minutes until cheese bubbles.

**Serves 4.**

*Can serve as entrée with favorite pasta sauce and Italian bread.*

# Kay's Potato Casserole

6 medium potatoes
1 pint sour cream
10 ounces sharp Cheddar
  cheese, grated
8-10 green onions, chopped
3 tablespoons milk
1 teaspoon salt
¼ teaspoon black pepper
¼ cup butter or margarine,
  melted

1.  Preheat oven to 350°.
2.  Boil potatoes, cool, peel, and shred on cheese grater.
3.  Mix all ingredients well and pour into 13" x 9" x 2" casserole and bake at 350° about 30-40 minutes until bubbling.

**Serves 6.**

*Sprinkle with chopped fresh parsley.*

# MAKE-AHEAD MASHED POTATOES

8-10 large potatoes
½ cup margarine
6 ounces cream cheese, softened
1 cup sour cream
4 ounces shredded Cheddar cheese
½ cup grated Parmesan cheese
4 green onions, chopped
1 tablespoon salt
1 teaspoon pepper

1. Preheat oven to 350°.
2. Peel and cook potatoes, drain, and mash while hot.
3. Add remaining ingredients, beating well.
4. Turn into greased 3-quart casserole and bake at 350° for 45 minutes.
5. Cover and refrigerate up to 2 weeks.

**Serves 8-10.**

# ROASTED NEW POTATOES

6 pounds red new potatoes, scrubbed and halved
8 garlic cloves, minced
1½ cups extra virgin olive oil
1 large bunch cilantro, basil, or mint, stems removed and chopped
1 tablespoon coarse salt, less if desired
Fresh ground pepper to taste

1. Preheat oven to 400°.
2. In large bowl, toss potatoes with all other ingredients. Place in shallow roasting pan and roast for about 1½ to 2 hours.

**Serves 8-10.**

*Wonderful with grilled meats and fish.*

# STUFFED HERBED POTATOES

16 red new potatoes,
scrubbed
5 tablespoons and 2
tablespoons butter, room
temperature
1½ cups chopped cabbage
1 small onion, minced
6 ounces cream cheese, room
temperature
2 tablespoons sour cream
2 ounces Gruyère cheese,
grated
3 tablespoons minced parsley
3 green onions, minced
1 large garlic clove, minced
Salt and pepper to taste

1. Preheat oven to 400°.

2. Bake potatoes at 400° for 1 hour. When cool, cut crosswise in half and carefully scoop out pulp, leaving ⅛" to ¼" shell.

3. In large bowl, mash potato pulp and add 5 tablespoons of butter. Set aside.

4. In skillet, heat 2 tablespoons butter and sauté cabbage and onion until translucent. Mix into mashed potato.

5. Beat cream cheese and sour cream until fluffy. Add Gruyère, parsley, green onions, and garlic.

6. Mix two-thirds of cheese mixture into mashed potatoes and season with salt and pepper. Spoon into potato shells and press two shells together.

7. Arrange potatoes on sides in greased baking dish. Spoon remaining cheese mixture over each potato.

8. Cover and chill in refrigerator at least 1 hour. When ready to bake, preheat oven to 325° and bake 20 minutes.

**Serves 8.**

*May prepare up to 2 days ahead and refrigerate until ready to bake.*

*Also great as appetizer.*

# PUFFED POTATO WEDGES

3 Idaho potatoes
Bacon fat or oil to coat skins
Salt

1. Preheat oven to 425°.

2. Wash potatoes, dry, and rub skins with oil. Cut each potato into 8 wedges, being careful to keep water away from the meat of the potato.

3. Sprinkle salt on cut sides of each wedge. Arrange wedges on wire rack and let stand 20 minutes.

4. Place wedges directly on oven rack (with a baking sheet on rack below to catch juices) and bake at 425° for 20 minutes until brown.

**Serves 4.**

# FRENCH FRIES WITHOUT FRYING

4 medium potatoes
1 tablespoon oil
Salt to taste

1. Preheat oven to 475°.

2. Peel potatoes and cut into long strips about ½" wide. Dry strips thoroughly on paper towels.

3. In bowl, toss potato strips with oil, coating thoroughly.

4. Spread potato strips on cookie sheet in single layer and bake at 475° for 35 minutes, turning to brown on all sides.

5. Sprinkle with salt before serving.

**Serves 6.**

*For crispier potato, broil last few minutes.*

# SWEET POTATO CASSEROLE

3 cups mashed sweet potatoes
1 cup sugar
¼ cup evaporated milk
2 eggs, beaten
1 teaspoon vanilla extract
1 stick margarine, cubed
1 cup coconut

**TOPPING**
1 cup chopped nuts
1 cup brown sugar
1 stick margarine, softened
½ cup flour

1. Preheat oven to 300°.
2. Peel and cube sweet potatoes. Boil until tender, then mash.
3. Add next 6 ingredients and mix with electric mixer. Pour into greased 8" x 8" x 2" baking dish or loaf pan.
4. Mix topping ingredients and crumble on top of potato mixture.
5. Bake at 300° for 30 minutes.

**Serves 6-8.**

*Great with poultry.*

# THANKSGIVING MEDLEY

3 large sweet potatoes or
   yams
¼ cup margarine or butter
½ cup brown sugar
6-8 ounces fresh cranberries
½ cup golden raisins
Pecans (optional)

1. Preheat oven to 400°.
2. Peel and quarter sweet potatoes lengthwise. Place in greased 12" x 9" x 2" glass dish.
3. Top with margarine or butter and brown sugar. Bake at 400° for 30 minutes.
4. Add cranberries and raisins, reduce heat to 350°, and continue baking another hour until potatoes are tender.
5. Top with pecans if desired.

**Serves 4-6.**

# PARSLEY PIE

1 cup rice
1 small onion, chopped
2 eggs, beaten
½ cup vegetable oil
¼ cup dried parsley flakes
½ pound sharp Cheddar cheese, grated
1 cup evaporated milk

1.  Preheat oven to 250°.
2.  Cook rice according to package directions.
3.  Add all other ingredients to rice and place in 13″ x 9″ x 2″ baking dish. Bake at 250° for 1 hour.

**Serves 12-14.**

*Miers' family holiday tradition.*

# JALAPEÑO CORN & RICE CASSEROLE

1 cup rice
1 medium onion, chopped
1 medium green pepper, chopped
1 cup chopped celery
½ cup butter or margarine, melted
1 tablespoon sugar
1-2 jalapeño peppers, finely chopped
2 (7-ounce) cans cream-style corn
1 cup shredded mild Cheddar cheese

1.  Preheat oven to 350°.
2.  Cook rice according to package directions; set aside.
3.  Sauté onion, green pepper, and celery in butter until tender.
4.  Combine rice, vegetables, sugar, jalapeño peppers, and corn. Spoon into greased 8″ x 10″ baking dish and top with cheese.
5.  Bake at 325° for 25 minutes.

**Serves 8-10.**

*All your friends will want this recipe.*

# FELZER'S RICE CASSEROLE

1 stick margarine
1 medium onion, finely
 chopped
10 mushrooms, sliced
2 cups raw white rice
2 (13¾-ounce) cans chicken
 consommé
1 cup white wine

1. Melt margarine in large skillet
 and slowly sauté onions and
 mushrooms.

2. Add rice and stir with fork to
 keep rice from sticking together.
 Add consommé, and white wine.

3. Cover and cook on medium heat
 about 20-30 minutes until liquid
 has soaked in. Fluff and serve.

**Serves 8-10.**

*May freeze leftovers in freezer
bags and reheat in microwave.*

# MIDLAND DIRTY RICE

8 green onions with tops,
 chopped
¾ stick margarine
1 cup raw brown rice
1 teaspoon oregano
1 (4-ounce) jar mushrooms
 plus liquid
1 teaspoon crushed red
 pepper flakes (optional)
1 (13¾-ounce) can beef broth
1 can water

1. Preheat oven to 350°.

2. Sauté green onions in margarine.
 When soft, add next 4 ingredients.

3. Pour broth and water into 8" x
 8" x 2" Pyrex dish. Stir in rice
 mixture, then bake at 350° for 2
 hours.

**Serves 6.**

# TARRANT DIRTY RICE

¾ stick butter or margarine
1¼ cups raw white rice
1 (10¾-ounce) can onion soup
1 (10½-ounce) can beef consommé
1 (4-ounce) jar mushrooms with liquid
1 tablespoon Worcestershire sauce
2 bay leaves

1. Preheat oven to 350°.
2. Melt butter in 8" x 8" x 2" glass baking dish and stir in rice.
3. Stir in remaining ingredients. Bake at 350° for 45 minutes to 1 hour.

**Serves 4-5.**

*Very easy and very tasty (even if you cut down on the butter).*

# RITZY RICE

2 cups uncooked instant rice
1 pound Monterey Jack cheese, grated
2 cups sour cream
2 (4-ounce) cans green chilies with juice
Salt to taste

1. Preheat oven to 350°.
2. Combine all ingredients together and place in 13" x 9" x 2" glass baking dish.
3. Cover and bake at 350° for 30 minutes.

**Serves 8.**

# SPECIAL WILD RICE

½ medium onion, chopped
1 (4½-ounce) jar sliced
 mushrooms, drained
1 stick butter or margarine
½ cup Uncle Ben's Long
 Grain Rice
¼ cup wild rice
1 teaspoon paprika
1 teaspoon dried oregano
1 bay leaf
Pepper to taste
1 (10½-ounce) can beef
 consommé with gelatin
½ cup cooking sherry
¾ cup water

1. Preheat oven to 375°.
2. Sauté onions and mushrooms in butter. Add long grain rice, wild rice, and spices. Reduce heat, cover, and simmer for 20 minutes.
3. Spray a 2-quart casserole with cooking oil spray. Combine simmered ingredients, consommé, sherry, and water in casserole dish.
4. Cover and bake at 375° for 45 minutes. Uncover and bake another 15-25 minutes until rice absorbs all liquids.

**Serves 4-6.**

*Wonderful with chicken, turkey, or ham at holiday festivities.*

# KAREN'S RICE PILAF

3 tablespoons butter or
 margarine
½ cup uncooked vermicelli,
 broken up
2 tablespoons pine nuts
2 cups chicken broth
1 cup raw long-grain rice

1. In heavy 2-quart saucepan, melt butter over moderate heat. Add vermicelli and brown. When almost brown, add pine nuts and brown.
2. Add chicken broth and bring to boil.
3. Add rice and reduce to low heat. Cover and simmer 20-25 minutes. Do not remove lid until done.

**Serves 4.**

# ORZO & PINE NUT PILAF

1 small onion, chopped
1 celery stalk, chopped
1 tablespoon olive oil
1 cup orzo pasta
2 cups chicken broth
1 chicken bouillon cube
3 tablespoons pine nuts
1 tablespoon minced parsley
Salt and pepper to taste
Grated Parmesan cheese to
    taste

1. Cook onion and celery in oil for about 8 minutes over medium heat, stirring until soft and beginning to brown.

2. Stir orzo into pan; mix well to coat pasta.

3. Add stock and bouillon cube. Bring to boil, then reduce heat and cover. Simmer for 15 minutes until pasta is cooked.

4. Stir in remaining ingredients.

**Serves 2-4.**

*May add finely diced tomato, carrot, or red pepper. Wonderful with grilled meats or poultry.*

# OYSTER BAKE

½ pound saltine crackers,
    crumbled fine
1 pint oysters, chopped, plus
    ¼ cup liquid
½ cup butter, melted
1 teaspoon salt
Red pepper to taste
¾ cup heavy cream

1. Preheat oven to 350°.

2. Combine 2 cups cracker crumbs with remaining ingredients.

3. Place in greased 1-quart casserole and sprinkle with extra cracker crumbs. Bake at 350° for 40 minutes.

**Serves 6-8.**

*Delicious with holiday turkey.*

DESSERTS

# ANISETTE COOKIES

2 eggs
4 egg yolks
1 cup sugar
2½ cups cake flour
2 teaspoons anise extract

1. Preheat oven to 375°.

2. Beat whole eggs, yolks, and sugar with electric mixture until foamy and lemon-colored.

3. Continue mixing on low, adding cake flour and anise extract. Dough will be shiny yellow and sticky.

4. Drop by teaspoonfuls onto greased cookie sheets. Bake at 375° for 15 minutes until light brown.

5. Cool on racks, store in airtight containers up to 1 month.

**Yields 3 dozen.**

*After baking, freeze up to 4 months.*

# GRANDMA'S OATMEAL COOKIES

1 cup butter, softened
1 cup brown sugar
1 cup granulated sugar
2 eggs
1 teaspoon vanilla extract
1½ cups flour
1 teaspoon salt
1 teaspoon soda
1 teaspoon cinnamon
3 cups quick-cooking oats
1 cup broken pecans
2 cups raisins or 1 (12-ounce) package chocolate chips

1. Preheat oven to 350°.

2. Cream butter and sugars. Stir in eggs and vanilla.

3. In separate bowl, sift together flour, salt, soda, and cinnamon. Gradually add to butter mixture.

4. Gradually stir in oats, then add pecans and either raisins or chocolate chips.

5. Drop by teaspoonfuls about 1" apart on greased cookie sheet.

6. Bake at 350° for 8-10 minutes.

**Yields 2-3 dozen.**

# ANZACS (AUSTRALIA, NEW ZEALAND, ARMY CORPS)

1 cup rolled oats
1 cup coconut
1 cup sugar
1 cup flour
⅓ cup butter
1 tablespoon molasses
2 tablespoons boiling water
1 teaspoon baking soda

1. Preheat oven to 300°.
2. Combine oats, coconut, sugar, and flour in a bowl.
3. In a saucepan, melt butter. Add molasses and water, then bring to boil.
4. Remove from heat and add baking soda. Pour over dry mixture and stir until combined.
5. Roll into balls and place on greased cookie sheet. Bake at 300° for 15-20 minutes.

**Yields 2 dozen.**

# THE '100' COOKIE

1 cup sugar
1 cup brown sugar, packed
1 cup margarine, softened
½ cup vegetable oil
1 egg
2 teaspoons vanilla extract
2 cups Special K cereal
1 cup coconut
1 cup quick-cooking oats
1 cup chopped pecans
¾ teaspoon salt
3½ cups flour
1 teaspoon baking soda
1 teaspoon cream of tartar

1. Preheat oven to 350°.
2. In a large bowl, combine first 10 ingredients.
3. Sift together salt, flour, soda, and cream of tartar. Add to sugar mixture and mix well.
4. Drop by teaspoonfuls onto greased cookie sheet. Bake at 350° for 10-12 minutes.

**Yields 6 dozen.**

*Can freeze dough in 6-ounce frozen juice cans or formed into long roll and wrapped in plastic wrap. Slice in ¼" thick slices when ready to bake.*

# BECKIE'S CHOCOLATE CHIP MACADAMIA NUT COOKIES

1 cup butter, softened
1/2 cup granulated sugar
1/2 cup brown sugar
1 teaspoon vanilla extract
1 teaspoon water
2 eggs
2 cups sifted flour
1 teaspoon baking soda
1 (3 1/2-ounce) jar macadamia nuts
1 (12-ounce) package real milk chocolate bits

1. Preheat oven to 350°.
2. Cream butter and sugars. Add eggs, vanilla, and water.
3. Sift together flour and baking soda. Add to wet ingredients, then add nuts and chocolate bits.
4. Form into balls of almost 1 tablespoonful and place on greased cookie sheet.
5. Bake at 350° for 10 minutes until bottoms are brown and center is chewy.

**Yields 2 dozen large cookies.**

*Dough may be prepared ahead and frozen.*

# AMISH SUGAR COOKIES

1 cup sugar
1 cup confectioners' sugar
1 cup butter or margarine, softened
1 cup oil
2 eggs
4 1/2 cups flour
1 teaspoon cream of tartar
1 teaspoon baking soda
1 teaspoon vanilla extract

1. Preheat oven to 375°.
2. Combine ingredients in order given. Roll into balls and bake on ungreased cookie sheet at 375° for 10-12 minutes.
3. Cool and sprinkle with more confectioners' sugar if desired.

**Yields 3 dozen.**

# MOLASSES SUGAR COOKIES

¾ cup vegetable shortening
1 cup and 2 tablespoons
   sugar
¼ cup molasses
1 egg
2 cups flour
2 teaspoons baking soda
½ teaspoon cloves
½ teaspoon ginger
1 teaspoon cinnamon
½ teaspoon salt
2 tablespoons sugar

1. Preheat oven to 375°.
2. Combine dry ingredients. Cream vegetable shortening, 1 cup sugar, molasses, and egg.
3. Add remaining dry ingredients and chill batter.
4. Sprinkle 2 tablespoons sugar on wax paper. Form dough into 1" balls and roll balls in sugar.
5. Place on greased cookie sheets and bake at 375° for about 8 minutes.

**Yields 3 dozen.**

*For chewy cookies, serve immediately.*

# POPPY ROUX'S TEA CAKES

1 cup butter, softened
1½ cups sugar
2 eggs
1 teaspoon vanilla extract
4 cups flour
1 teaspoon baking soda
Pinch of salt

1. Preheat oven to 325°.
2. Combine butter, sugar, and eggs one at a time. Add vanilla and beat well.
3. Sift flour, baking soda, and salt. Add dry ingredients one-third at a time to butter mixture.
4. Roll out dough on floured surface and cut into triangles. Bake at 325° for 12 minutes

**Yields 4 dozen cookies.**

*Wonderful holiday treat.*

# LACE COOKIES

1 cup flour
1 cup finely chopped pecans
½ cup light corn syrup
½ cup brown sugar, packed
1 stick butter
1 teaspoon vanilla extract

1.  Preheat oven to 350°.

2.  Mix flour and nuts, then set aside.

3.  Combine syrup, brown sugar, and butter in 4-quart saucepan. Bring to boil over medium heat, stirring constantly.

4.  Remove sugar mixture from heat and stir in flour mixture. Add vanilla and mix well.

5.  Drop by teaspoonfuls about 3" apart onto foil-covered cookie sheets. Bake at 350° for 8-10 minutes until golden.

6.  Cool 3-5 minutes until foil peels from cookie sheets easily. Move cookies to flat surface of paper towels or wire racks to dry.

**Yields 4 dozen.**

# GRANDMA TODEY'S BROWNIES

1 stick margarine
4 tablespoons cocoa powder
2 eggs
1 cup sugar
1 cup flour
1 teaspoon vanilla extract
½ cup chopped pecans or walnuts (optional)

1.  Preheat oven to 350°.

2.  Melt margarine in saucepan and stir in cocoa. Set aside.

3.  Mix together eggs, sugar, flour, and vanilla. Add chocolate mixture and nuts, if desired.

4.  Pour batter into 8" x 8" x 2" Pyrex dish and bake at 350° for about 30 minutes.

**Yields 1½ dozen.**

177

# JENNYE'S FROSTED BROWNIES

1 stick margarine or butter
1 cup sugar
4 eggs
1 teaspoon vanilla extract
½ teaspoon salt
1 (16-ounce) can chocolate
  syrup
1 cup plus 1 tablespoon flour
1 cup chopped nuts
1 cup mini-marshmallows

**FROSTING**

1½ cups sugar
6 tablespoons butter
6 tablespoons milk
Salt to taste
1 cup chocolate chips

1. Preheat oven to 350°.

2. Cream butter and sugar. Add eggs and beat well, then stir in next 5 ingredients.

3. Spread in 15" x 10" x 2" greased jelly-roll pan. Bake at 350° for 25-30 minutes.

4. While baking, prepare frosting: bring sugar, butter, milk, and salt to boil for 30 seconds. Stir in chocolate chips until melted.

5. Remove brownies from oven, sprinkle with marshmallows, and spread with warm frosting.

**Yields 2-3 dozen.**

# BUTTERSCOTCH BROWNIES

4 tablespoons melted butter
1 cup dark brown sugar
1 egg
½ teaspoon vanilla extract
¾ cup flour
1 teaspoon baking powder
¼ cup coconut
½ cup broken pecans

**CARAMEL ICING** (optional)

½ cup butter
½ cup dark brown sugar
¼ cup half-and-half (or milk)
1½-2 cups confectioners'
  sugar
1 teaspoon maple or vanilla
  extract

1. Preheat oven to 350°.

2. Cream butter, sugar, egg, and vanilla. Mix flour and baking powder; stir into sugar mixture. Add coconut and pecans.

3. Spread into greased 8" x 8" x 2" pan. Bake at 350° for 25 minutes, then cool.

4. Melt butter over low heat until caramel color. Add brown sugar and cook until sugar is melted.

5. Pour in half-and-half, cool to room temperature, then gradually beat in sugar and extract.

6. Beat vigorously until icing thickens. Spread on brownies.

**Yields 1½ dozen.**

# Butter Pecan Bars

1 stick butter or margarine
1 box yellow butter cake mix
3 eggs
1 (8-ounce) package cream cheese
1 (1-pound) box confectioners' sugar
1 cup chopped pecans

1. Preheat oven to 350°.
2. Melt butter in 13" x 9" x 2" pan. Add cake mix and 1 egg. Stir together with a fork to form crust.
3. Combine cream cheese, 2 eggs, and confectioners' sugar. Pour over crust.
4. Sprinkle with chopped pecans and bake at 350° for 40-45 minutes until golden brown. Cool and cut into squares.

**Yields 2 dozen.**

*Try chocolate cake mix for a different and great taste.*

# Raisin Bars

1 cup raisins
1 cup water
½ cup vegetable oil
1 cup sugar
1 egg
1¾ cups flour
¼ teaspoon salt
1 teaspoon soda
1 teaspoon cinnamon
½ teaspoon nutmeg
½ teaspoon allspice
¼ teaspoon cloves
½ cup chocolate chips
½ cup walnuts (optional)
½ cup confectioners' sugar

1. Preheat oven to 375°.
2. Bring raisins and water to boil in saucepan. Remove from heat, stir in oil, and cool to lukewarm. Stir in sugar and egg.
3. Sift together next 7 ingredients and beat into raisin mixture. Stir in chocolate chips and nuts.
4. Pour into greased 13" x 9" x 2" pan and bake at 375° for 20-25 minutes.
5. Dust lightly with confectioners' sugar and cut into squares.

**Yields 2 dozen.**

# CHOCOLATE CHIP CREME SQUARES

1 (34-ounce) roll chocolate chip cookie dough
2 (8-ounce) packages cream cheese, room temperature
1½ cups sugar
3 eggs
2 teaspoons vanilla extract

**ICING**
1 stick butter or margarine
3 heaping tablespoons cocoa powder
5 tablespoons evaporated milk
½-⅔ (1-pound) box confectioners' sugar
Chopped pecans (optional)

1. Preheat oven to 325°.
2. Slice cookie dough and pat lightly into 13" x 9" x 2" pan. Bake at 325° for 4 minutes until dough covers bottom of pan.
3. Mix cream cheese with sugar, beating until smooth. Add eggs one at a time, beating well after each. Stir in vanilla.
4. Pour mixture over cookie dough and bake at 325° for 30 minutes until mixture sets.
5. Prepare icing: Combine butter, cocoa powder, and evaporated milk. Heat, stirring constantly, until thickened.
6. Add confectioners' sugar and stir until spreading consistency. Spread over warm cookie mixture and sprinkle with pecans.
7. Cool, then cut into squares.

**Yields 1-1½ dozen.**

# Pumpkin Spice Squares

4 eggs
2 cups sugar
1 cup oil
1 (16-ounce) can pumpkin
2 cups flour
2 teaspoons baking powder
2 teaspoons cinnamon
1 teaspoon baking soda
¾ teaspoon salt
¼ teaspoon cloves
½ cup raisins

**Frosting**

3 ounces cream cheese
¼ cup plus 2 tablespoons
  margarine, softened
1 teaspoon vanilla extract
2 cups confectioners' sugar
½ cup chopped nuts
  (optional)

1. Preheat oven to 350°.
2. Beat eggs, sugar, oil, and pumpkin. Mix in remaining cake ingredients, adding raisins last.
3. Bake in a greased 15" x 10" x 2" jelly-roll pan at 350° for 20-30 minutes. Cool.
4. While baking, prepare icing: mix cream cheese, margarine, and vanilla. Stir in confectioners' sugar.
5. Frost pumpkin squares with icing, sprinkle with nuts, cut into squares, and refrigerate.

**Yields 3 dozen.**

# ALYCE'S APPLE CAKE

4 cups chopped apple,
  unpeeled
2 eggs, beaten
2 cups sugar
½ cup oil
2 cups sifted flour
2 teaspoons baking soda
2 teaspoons cinnamon
1 teaspoon salt
1 cup chopped pecans

**FROSTING**

1 (8-ounce) package cream
  cheese
1 stick butter, softened
1 teaspoon vanilla extract
1 (1-pound) box
  confectioners' sugar

1. Preheat oven to 350°.
2. Mix cake ingredients and bake in a lightly greased 13" x 9" x 2" pan at 350° for 50 minutes.
3. Combine all frosting ingredients, stirring until smooth. Spread on cooled cake.

**Serves 10-12.**

# 1-2-3-4 CAKE

1 cup margarine, softened
2 cups sugar
4 eggs, separated
1 tablespoon vanilla extract
3 cups flour
2 teaspoons baking powder
1 cup milk

**FROSTING**

6 very ripe bananas, mashed
½ cup butter, melted
About ¾ (1-pound) box
  confectioners' sugar
Dash of salt

1. Preheat oven to 325°.
2. Cream margarine and sugar. Beat in egg yolks and vanilla.
3. Mix flour and baking powder. Add to other ingredients, alternating with milk.
4. Beat egg whites until stiff and fold into mixture.
5. Place batter in 3 round pans or one 13" x 9" x 2" baking dish. Bake at 325° for 40-45 minutes.
6. Combine frosting ingredients, adding enough sugar to make thin frosting. Frost warm cake.

**Serves 6-8.**

# HEAVENLY BLUEBERRY CAKE

2 eggs, separated
1 cup sugar, divided
1/2 cup butter, softened
1/2 teaspoon salt
3/4 teaspoon vanilla or lemon
  extract
1 1/2 cups sifted flour
1 teaspoon baking powder
1/3 cup milk
1 1/2 cups blueberries, washed
  and floured
1 teaspoon cinnamon
2 teaspoons sugar

1. Preheat oven to 350°.

2. Beat whites, gradually adding 1/2 cup of sugar until soft peaks form. Set aside.

3. Cream butter, gradually adding salt and remaining sugar. Add vanilla and unbeaten yolks. Beat until creamy.

4. Sift flour and baking powder. Alternately add flour mixture and milk to creamed mixture, beginning and ending with flour.

5. Fold in berries. Fold in 1/3 of egg white to lighten batter. Fold in remaining egg whites.

6. Turn into greased 8" x 8" x 2" pan. Combine cinnamon and sugar and sprinkle on cake.

7. Bake at 350° for 50 minutes until cake is a golden brown with crisp crust.

**Serves 10.**

*Won't be around long!*

# HEAVENLY SHORTCAKE

2 cups flour
4 teaspoons baking powder
½ teaspoon salt
½ cup sugar
4 tablespoons melted butter
¾ cup milk
1 egg, beaten
Lightly sugared strawberries, peaches, blueberries, and/or raspberries
Whipped cream

1. Preheat oven to 425°.
2. Sift together flour, baking powder, salt, and sugar.
3. Melt butter and stir in milk and egg. Add to dry ingredients.
4. Pat into greased 9" x 1½" pie plate and bake at 425° for 25 minutes.
5. Cut into wedges, split each horizontally and butter if desired.
6. Place fruit over bottom half of cake wedge and top with other half. Cover with more fruit and whipped cream.

**Serves 6-8.**

*Best if cake is warm.*

# CHOP SUEY CAKE

2 cups flour
2 cups sugar
2 eggs
2 teaspoons baking soda
1 cup chopped walnuts
1 (20-ounce) can crushed pineapple, with juice

**ICING**

1 (8-ounce) package cream cheese
1 stick butter, softened
2 cups confectioners' sugar
1 teaspoon vanilla extract

1. Preheat oven to 350°.
2. Combine all cake ingredients with spoon. Pour into greased 12" x 9" x 2" pan and bake at 350° for 40 minutes.
3. As cake cooks, prepare icing: blend ingredients well with electric mixer.
4. Pour icing over hot cake. Chill 24 hours before serving.

**Serves 12.**

# Austrian Plum Cake

2 cups flour
½ cup sugar
2 teaspoons baking powder
½ teaspoon salt
¾ stick unsalted (sweet) butter, cold and cut into pieces
1 large egg
½ cup milk

**TOPPING**

2 pounds (about 30) purple (Italian) plums, halved and pitted
¾ cup sugar
1 teaspoon cinnamon
⅛ teaspoon freshly grated nutmeg
2 tablespoons unsalted (sweet) butter, melted
4 tablespoons fresh lemon juice
½ cup confectioners' sugar

1. Preheat oven to 350°.
2. In large mixing bowl, whisk together first 4 dry ingredients.
3. Add butter and blend until mixture resembles meal
4. Whisk together egg and milk. Add to flour mixture, stirring just to combine.
5. With well-floured hands, press batter evenly into buttered 15½" x 12½" jelly-roll pan.
6. With cut side up, arrange plums tightly together over batter covering completely.
7. Combine sugar, cinnamon and nutmeg. Sprinkle over plums, then drizzle with butter and lemon juice.
8. Cover cake with buttered piece of wax paper, secured in each corner with toothpick. Bake in middle of 350° oven for 30 to 35 minutes until plums are cooked through and bubbly.
9. When done, discard wax paper. Let cake cool on rack for 5 minutes, then sift confectioners' sugar on top. Serve cake warm or at room temperature.

**Serves 15.**

*May substitute other fruit like thinly sliced apples or peaches, or pitted and halved cherries or apricots.*

# CAJUN CAKE

2 cups flour
1½ cups sugar
1 teaspoon baking soda
2 eggs
1 (15¼-ounce) can crushed
   pineapple, with juice

**ICING**
¾ cup sugar
½ cup evaporated milk
1 stick butter or margarine,
   softened
1 (3½-ounce) can coconut
1 cup pecans

1. Preheat oven to 350°.
2. Combine cake ingredients. Pour into greased 11" x 7" x 2" pan and bake at 350° for 30-35 minutes.
3. As cake cooks, combine icing ingredients. Cook for 5 minutes over medium-high heat. Spread on hot cake.

**Serves 8-10.**

*Nice ending to meal of gumbo and dilly bread.*

# CREOLE CAKE

2 eggs
½ cup cooking oil
½ cup buttermilk
1 teaspoon vanilla extract
2 cups sugar
2 tablespoons cocoa powder
1 teaspoon baking soda
2 cups flour
1 cup boiling water

**TOPPING**
1 stick butter, melted
1 (3½-ounce) can coconut
1 (5-ounce) can evaporated
   milk
1 (1-pound) box light brown
   sugar
½ cup chopped nuts
1 teaspoon vanilla extract

1. Preheat oven to 350°.
2. Mix ingredients for cake in order given.
3. Pour into greased and floured 16" x 11" x 2" pan and bake at 350° for 30 minutes.
4. As cake cooks, mix all topping ingredients well.
5. Pour over hot cake, then place under broiler until bubbling.
6. Cool cake and cut into squares.

**Serves 8-10.**

*Topping can be used on many different cakes.*

# GRIZZLE'S SPICE CAKE

4 eggs
2 cups sugar
1 cup vegetable oil
1 (16-ounce) can refried
 beans
2 cups flour
1 teaspoon salt
2 teaspoons baking soda
2 teaspoons baking powder
2 teaspoons cinnamon
1/8 teaspoon cloves
1/8 teaspoon ginger
1 teaspoon nutmeg
1 cup chopped nuts
1/2 cup coconut
1 teaspoon vanilla extract

**CREAM CHEESE ICING** (optional)

1 stick butter, room
 temperature
1 (8-ounce) package cream
 cheese, room temperature
1 (1-pound) box
 confectioners' sugar

1.  Preheat oven to 375°.

2.  Add eggs to sugar, one at a time, then add oil and beans. Stir to moisten.

3.  Stir in remaining ingredients.

4.  Pour into 3 greased and floured 9" cake pans and bake at 375° for 25-30 minutes.

5.  For icing, thoroughly mix butter and cream cheese. Gradually stir in confectioners' sugar. Spread between layers and on top of cooled cake.

**Serves 8-10.**

# MEXICAN SHEET CAKE

2 cups sugar
2 cups flour
¼ teaspoon salt
2 sticks butter or margarine
4 tablespoons cocoa powder
1 cup water
¼ teaspoon baking soda
½ cup buttermilk
2 eggs, slightly beaten

**ICING**

1 stick butter or margarine
4 tablespoons cocoa powder
6 tablespoons milk
1 (1-pound) box
  confectioners' sugar
1 teaspoon vanilla extract
1 cup chopped pecans

1.  Preheat oven to 400°.

2.  Sift sugar, flour, and salt. In saucepan, bring margarine, cocoa, and water to boil. Pour over flour mixture and mix well.

3.  Add soda, buttermilk, and eggs. Mix well and pour into greased 15" x 10" x 2" jelly-roll pan. Bake at 400° for 20 minutes.

4.  During last 5 minutes of baking, prepare icing: bring butter, cocoa, and milk to boil. Remove from heat and add sugar, vanilla, and pecans. Beat well and spread on hot cake.

**Serves 15.**

# BETINA'S CARROT CAKE

1½ cups oil
2 cups sugar
4 eggs
1 teaspoon vanilla extract
2 cups flour
2 teaspoons cinnamon
2 teaspoons baking powder
2 teaspoons baking soda
3 cups grated carrots
1 cup chopped pecans

**ICING**

1 (8-ounce) package cream
  cheese, softened
1 stick butter, softened
1 (1-pound) box
  confectioners' sugar

1.  Preheat oven to 350°.

2.  Combine oil and sugar, beating well. Add eggs, one at time and beating well after each. Stir in vanilla.

3.  Sift together flour, cinnamon, baking powder, and soda. Stir in egg mixture.

4.  Fold in carrots and pecans. Pour into greased 13" x 9" x 2" pan and bake at 350° for 45 minutes.

5.  For icing, cream together cream cheese, butter, and sugar until smooth. Spread on cooled cake.

**Serves 16.**

188

# CHOCOLATE CHIP CARROT CAKE

4 eggs
2 cups sugar
1½ cups oil
3 cups flour
2 teaspoons cinnamon
2 teaspoons baking powder
2 teaspoons baking soda
½ teaspoon salt
2 (6-ounce) jars junior baby
  food carrots
1 cup chocolate chips
1 cup chopped nuts

**FROSTING**

3 ounces cream cheese,
  softened
3 tablespoons milk
1 teaspoon vanilla extract
2½ cups confectioners' sugar

1. Preheat oven to 350°.

2. Beat together eggs, sugar, and oil.

3. Sift dry ingredients. Slowly add to egg mixture.

4. Mix in carrots, chocolate chips, and nuts.

5. Pour batter into greased and floured tube pan. Bake at 350° for 1 hour.

6. Cool ½ hour before removing from pan and cool completely before frosting.

7. To make frosting, blend cheese, milk, and vanilla. Gradually add sugar until smooth, adding teaspoons of milk if necessary.

**Serves 12-16.**

*May add grated carrots to batter or as garnish for top.*

# BLACK BOTTOM CUPCAKES

**TOPPING**

2 (8-ounce) packages cream cheese
1 egg
⅔ cup sugar
1 teaspoon salt
1 (12-ounce) package semi-sweet chocolate chips

**CUPCAKES**

1½ cups flour
1 cup sugar
¼ cup cocoa powder
1 teaspoon baking soda
½ teaspoon salt
½ cup oil
1 cup water
1 tablespoon vinegar
1 teaspoon vanilla extract

1. Preheat oven to 350°.

2. In bowl, combine topping ingredients, beat well, then set aside.

3. For cupcakes, sift together dry ingredients. Add remaining ingredients and beat well.

4. Either grease muffin tins or use cupcake liners. Fill each ⅓ full with batter and a heaping tablespoonful of topping.

5. Bake at 350° for 30 minutes until golden brown.

**Yields 2 dozen.**

*Great for children's parties, but adults love them too!*

# TEXAS FUDGE CAKE

4 eggs
2 cups sugar
1 cup flour
6 tablespoons cocoa powder
Pinch of salt
½ cup butter or margarine, melted
1 teaspoon vanilla extract

1. Preheat oven to 350°.

2. Combine all ingredients and pour into greased and floured 8" x 8" x 2" pan.

3. Bake at 350° for 20-25 minutes, removing from oven while center is slightly soft.

**Serves 12-16.**

# RHONDA'S FAVORITE CHOCOLATE CAKE

2 eggs
1 cup buttermilk
3 cups flour
2 cups sugar
3 teaspoons baking soda
1 teaspoon salt
1 cup vegetable oil
1 teaspoon vanilla extract
1/4 cup cocoa powder
1 cup boiling water
**FROSTING**
1/2 cup butter, melted
1/2 cup cocoa powder
1 (1-pound) box
  confectioners' sugar
1 teaspoon vanilla extract
Milk for thinning

1. Preheat oven to 350°.
2. Beat eggs and add buttermilk. Add remaining cake ingredients and mix with spoon.
3. Place batter in greased and floured 13" x 9" x 2" pan or 2 round cake pans. Bake at 350° for 30 minutes.
4. Beat all frosting ingredients with mixer until smooth and creamy, gradually adding milk until spreadable consistency. Frost cake when cooled.

**Serves 12-16.**

# MISSISSIPPI MUD

2 cups sugar
1 cup butter or margarine, softened
4 eggs
1/2 cup flour
1/3 cup cocoa powder
1/4 teaspoon salt
3 teaspoons vanilla extract
1 cup chopped pecans
1/2 (10-ounce) package
  miniature marshmallows

1. Preheat oven to 300°.
2. Cream sugar and butter. Add eggs and beat by hand.
3. Sift flour, cocoa, and salt. Add to creamed mixture and mix well. Add vanilla and pecans.
4. Pour into greased and floured 11" x 7" x 2" pan. Bake at 300° for 35 minutes.
5. Remove cake from oven and cover with marshmallows.
6. Increase oven to 350° and return cake for 10 minutes. Cool 1 hour before serving.

**Serves 8-10.**

# CHOCOLATE ÉCLAIR CAKE

1 (1-pound) box graham crackers
2 (3⅝-ounce) packages instant French vanilla pudding
3 cups milk
1 (8-ounce) tub Cool Whip

**TOPPING**

2 ounces unsweetened chocolate squares, melted
2 tablespoons light corn syrup
2 teaspoons vanilla extract
3 tablespoons butter, softened
3 tablespoons milk
1½ cups confectioners' sugar

1. Butter bottom and sides of 13" x 9" x 2" pan. Line with whole graham crackers.

2. Beat together pudding with milk. Add thawed Cool Whip and mix well.

3. Over bed of graham crackers, layer half the pudding mixture, graham crackers, remaining pudding, and more crackers.

4. Beat together topping ingredients and pour over all.

5. Refrigerate at least 24 hours! Cut into squares and enjoy.

**Serves 16.**

# ROCKY ROAD CAKE

12 ounces semi-sweet chocolate chips
¼ cup sugar
4 large eggs, separated
1 teaspoon vanilla extract
2 cups heavy cream
1 10" round angel food cake, torn into bite-sized pieces
1 cup chopped walnuts

1. Melt chocolate chips in double boiler. Add sugar. Mix in yolks slowly and thoroughly. Add vanilla and remove from heat.

2. Beat egg whites until stiff, but not dry. Fold into chocolate mixture.

3. Beat cream to soft peaks. Fold into chocolate mixture.

4. Grease 10" springform pan. Layer with with one-third of the cake pieces, one-third chocolate mixture, then one-third walnuts. Repeat twice.

5. Refrigerate overnight, remove from pan, and freeze until served.

**Serves 12.**

# MARMIE'S RED VELVET CAKE

½ cup vegetable shortening
1½ cups sugar
2 eggs
2 ounces red food coloring
2 tablespoons cocoa powder
2½ cups flour
1 teaspoon salt
1 cup buttermilk
1 teaspoon vanilla extract
¼ cup water
1 teaspoon baking soda
1 teaspoon vinegar

**ICING**
6 tablespoons flour
1½ cups milk
3 sticks butter (do not
   substitute margarine)
1½ cups sugar
1½ tablespoons vanilla
   extract

1. Preheat oven to 350°.

2. To make cake: cream shortening and sugar until fluffy. Add eggs and blend well.

3. Make a paste of food coloring and cocoa powder. Blend into shortening mixture.

4. Sift flour and salt together. To shortening mixture, add flour mixture alternating with buttermilk, vanilla, and water.

5. Add soda and blend well. Stir in vinegar, but do not beat.

6. Pour into 2 lightly greased 9" x 2" cake pans and bake at 350° for 20-30 minutes. Cool and split in halves to make 4 layers.

7. For icing, mix flour and milk in saucepan. Cook over low heat until thickened to pudding consistency.

8. Remove from heat and stir until room temperature (very important step).

9. Cream butter, sugar, and vanilla until fluffy. Add cooled flour and milk mixture and beat well for 10 minutes. Spread between layers and on top of cake.

**Serves 12-16.**

*Louisiana family tradition at Thanksgiving and Christmas.*

# MIGG'S POPPY SEED CAKE

1 yellow butter cake mix
1/2 cup sugar
3/4 cup vegetable oil
1/4 cup poppy seeds
1 cup sour cream
4 eggs
Confectioners' sugar

1. Preheat oven to 350°.
2. Combine first 3 ingredients. Add poppy seeds and sour cream. Add eggs, one at a time, mixing well.
3. Generously butter a 10" x 3½" Bundt pan and sprinkle with sugar.
4. Pour batter in Bundt pan and bake at 350° for 45-60 minutes until toothpick comes out clean. Dust with confectioners' sugar.

**Serves 12-14.**

*For a tasty alternative, use lemon cake mix and 1 teaspoon lemon extract.*

# KELLEY'S POPPY SEED CAKE

1 box white cake mix
1 tablespoon almond extract
1 (6-ounce) package instant
  vanilla pudding
5 eggs
1/2 cup orange juice
1/2 cup water
1/2 cup oil
2 tablespoons poppy seeds
**ICING**
Orange juice
1 cup confectioners' sugar

1. Preheat oven to 350°.
2. Combine all cake ingredients and beat for 5 minutes.
3. Pour in greased and floured 10" x 3½" Bundt pan and bake at 350° for 45 minutes.
4. Slowly add orange juice to confectioners' sugar until thin icing.
5. After baking, poke holes in cake with toothpick and dribble icing over hot cake.

**Yields 16-20 slices.**

# Chocolate Pound Cake

4 cups sifted cake flour
½ cup cocoa powder
¼ teaspoon baking powder
½ pound butter, softened
½ cup vegetable shortening
3 cups sugar
5 eggs
1¼ cups whole milk
1 teaspoon vanilla extract

**Icing**

2 cups sugar
¼ cup cocoa powder
⅔ cup vegetable shortening
¼ teaspoon salt
⅔ cup milk
1 teaspoon vanilla extract

1. Preheat oven to 300°.
2. Sift first 3 ingredients together.
3. In large mixing bowl, cream butter, vegetable shortening, and sugar until light and fluffy. Beat in eggs one at a time.
4. Fold in dry ingredients alternating with milk. Add vanilla.
5. Pour batter into greased and floured 10" x 3½" Bundt pan or 13" x 9" x 2" pan.
6. Bake at 300° for about 1 hour and 25 minutes until toothpick comes out clean. Cool before icing.
7. In saucepan, add all icing ingredients except vanilla. Boil fast 2 minutes, stirring constantly. Do not overcook.
8. Remove from heat and add vanilla. Beat until creamy. Pour over cooled cake.

**Yields 16 slices or 20 squares.**

*For brownie-like texture, use ¾ cup milk.*

# OLD FASHIONED POUND CAKE

1 pound butter, softened
3 cups sugar
6 eggs
4 cups sifted flour
¾ cup whole milk
1 teaspoon almond extract
1 teaspoon vanilla extract

1. Preheat oven to 300°.
2. In large mixing bowl, cream butter and sugar. Beat in eggs one at a time.
3. Fold in flour alternating with milk. Add extracts.
4. Pour batter into greased and floured 10" x 4" tube pan. Bake at 300° for 1 hour and 10 to 30 minutes, depending on oven, until toothpick comes out clean.
5. Serve with fresh fruit and whipped cream.

**Yields about 16 slices.**

# CREAM CHEESE POUND CAKE

3 sticks butter, softened
1 (8-ounce) package cream cheese
3 cups sugar
1½ teaspoons vanilla extract
Pinch of salt
6 eggs
3 cups sifted flour

1. Preheat oven to 325°.
2. In large mixing bowl, cream butter, cream cheese, and sugar. Add vanilla and salt.
3. Beat in eggs one at a time. Gradually add flour and mix well.
4. Pour batter into greased and floured 10" x 3½" Bundt pan and bake at 325° for about 1½ hours.

**Yields 16-20 slices.**

*Delicious with fresh berries.*

# SOUR CREAM POUND CAKE

½ pound butter, softened
3 cups sugar
6 eggs
3 cups flour
¼ teaspoon salt
¼ teaspoon baking soda
1 cup sour cream
1 teaspoon vanilla extract
2 teaspoons lemon extract

1. Preheat oven to 325°.
2. In large mixing bowl, cream butter and sugar. Beat in eggs one at a time.
3. Sift flour, salt, and baking soda together 3 times.
4. Add flour mixture, alternating with sour cream, beginning and ending with flour.
5. Add extracts. Pour batter into greased and floured 10" x 4" tube pan and bake at 325° for about 1 to 1½ hours. Do not open oven for first hour.

**Yields 16-20 slices.**

*Delicious with fruit, chocolate, or lemon sauce.*

*This cake mails well.*

# WHIPPING CREAM POUND CAKE

2 sticks butter or margarine, softened
3 cups sugar
6 eggs
3 cups sifted cake flour
1 teaspoon vanilla extract
1 cup heavy cream

1. Preheat oven to 300°.
2. In large mixing bowl, cream butter and sugar. Beat in eggs one at a time.
3. Stir in flour and add vanilla. Whip cream and fold in.
4. Pour batter into greased and floured 10" x 4" tube pan and bake at 300° for about 1½ hours.

**Yields 16-20 slices.**

# Rum Cake

½ cup chopped pecans
1 box butter cake mix
1 (3⅝-ounce) package instant
   vanilla pudding
4 eggs
½ cup rum
½ cup oil
½ cup water

**SAUCE**
½ cup butter
1 cup sugar
¼ cup rum
¼ cup water

1. Preheat oven to 350°.
2. Grease and flour 10" x 3½" Bundt pan. Sprinkle chopped pecans in bottom of pan.
3. Mix cake ingredients thoroughly. Pour into pan and bake at 350° for 45-50 minutes.
4. Heat sauce ingredients until sugar dissolved and sauce smooth.
5. Prick holes in cake with toothpick and pour sauce over hot cake.
6. Remove cake from pan after cooling to room temperature.

**Serves 12-16.**

*Nice housewarming gift.*

# Harvey Wallbanger Cake

1 yellow cake mix
1 cup oil
¼ cup Galliano liqueur
¼ cup vodka
1 (3⅝-ounce) package instant
   vanilla pudding
4 eggs
¼ cup orange juice

**GLAZE**
2 tablespoons butter, melted
2 cups confectioners' sugar
4 tablespoons orange juice

1. Preheat oven to 350°.
2. Combine all cake ingredients. Pour into greased 10" x 3½" Bundt pan and bake at 350° for 45-50 minutes.
3. Cool in pan 20 minutes, then remove from pan to cool to room temperature.
4. Combine glaze ingredients, adding more juice if necessary, and drizzle over cake.

**Serves 10-12.**

# BLACKBERRY WINE CAKE

1 cup chopped pecans,
  divided
1/2 cup blackberry wine
1/2 cup water
4 eggs
1 butter-fudge cake mix
1/2 cup oil
1 (3⅝-ounce) package instant
  vanilla pudding

### SYRUP

1 stick butter
1 cup sugar
1/4 cup blackberry wine
1/4 cup water

1. Preheat oven to 350°.
2. Sprinkle 1/2 cup pecans in bottom of greased 10" x 3½" Bundt pan.
3. Beat until creamy remaining cake ingredients, except pecans.
4. Fold in remaining pecans. Pour batter into pan and bake at 350° for 50-60 minutes.
5. Toward end of baking time, boil syrup ingredients in saucepan for 5 minutes. Pour over hot cake after baking.
6. Allow cake to cool in pan at least 2 hours before removing. Refrigerate.

**Serves 15-20.**

# FOOL-PROOF CHEESECAKE

### CRUST

1¾ cups graham cracker
  crumbs
1/4 cup chopped pecans
1/2 teaspoon nutmeg
1/2 cup melted butter

### FILLING

4 eggs, well beaten
2 (8-ounce) packages cream
  cheese
1 cup sugar
1/4 teaspoon salt
2 teaspoons vanilla extract
1/2 teaspoon almond extract
3 cups sour cream

1. Preheat oven to 375°.
2. Combine ingredients for crust and press on side and bottom of 9½" x 2½" springform pan.
3. Combine filling ingredients except sour cream. Beat until smooth, then add sour cream.
4. Pour filling into crust and bake at 375° for 35 minutes until set.
5. Cool 4-5 hours before removing springform. Refrigerate if not serving immediately.

**Serves 8-10.**

# OREO CHEESECAKE

## GRAHAM CRACKER CRUST

1¼ cups graham cracker crumbs

⅓ cup butter or margarine, melted

¼ cup firmly packed dark brown sugar

## FILLING

2 pounds cream cheese, softened

1¼ cups sugar

2 tablespoons flour

4 large eggs

2 large egg yolks

⅓ cup heavy cream

1 teaspoon vanilla

2 teaspoons crème de cacao

1½ cups coarsely chopped Oreos

## SOUR CREAM TOPPING

2 cups sour cream

¼ cup sugar

1 teaspoon vanilla

## SWISS FUDGE GLAZE

1 cup heavy cream

8 ounces semi-sweet chocolate, chopped

1 teaspoon vanilla

Oreos for garnish

## DAY ONE

1. Preheat oven to 425°.

2. Combine crust ingredients and press into bottom and 1" up sides of 10" springform pan. Refrigerate 30 minutes until firm.

3. In large bowl, prepare filling. Beat cream cheese on low speed. Add sugar and flour until blended. Add eggs and yolks, beating until smooth.

4. Stir in cream, vanilla, and crème de cacao.

5. Pour half the filling onto crust. Sprinkle with chopped Oreos, then cover with remaining filling and smooth with spatula.

6. Bake at 425° for 15 minutes, then reduce temperature to 225° and bake another 65 minutes.

7. Blend ingredients for topping. Spread over cake and bake another 7 minutes. Refrigerate overnight.

## DAY TWO

1. To prepare glaze, scald cream in heavy saucepan. Add chocolate and vanilla and stir for 1 minute. Remove from heat and stir until smooth.

2. Pour glaze over cake and press Oreo halves, cut side down, around edge.

**Serves 12.**

# RICOTTA CHEESE PIE

## CRUST

8 tablespoons vegetable
  shortening
4 tablespoons sugar
4 eggs
2 cups flour
2 teaspoons baking powder

## FILLING

5 eggs
2¼ cups sugar
Zest and juice of 1 lemon
3 pounds ricotta cheese
Cinnamon (optional)

1. Preheat oven to 350°.

2. Cream vegetable shortening and sugar. Add eggs and mix.

3. Gradually add flour and baking powder. (Consistency will be soft and gooey.)

4. Form into ball, place in wax paper, and refrigerate 1 hour.

5. Roll dough on floured surface and place in 13" x 9" x 2" baking dish. Crimp edges.

6. To make filling, separate 5 eggs. Beat egg whites and set aside.

7. Cream egg yolks and sugar. Add grated lemon rind and juice.

8. Beat ricotta cheese until creamy and add to filling mixture. Fold in egg whites.

9. Pour into crust and bake at 350° for 60-75 minutes until firm. Sprinkle with cinnamon when done.

**Serves 16.**

# BROWN BAG APPLE PIE

1¼ cups sugar
6 tablespoons flour
1 teaspoon cinnamon
¼ teaspoon nutmeg
6 large Granny Smith apples,
  sliced
1 9" unbaked pie shell
**TOPPING**
½ cup sugar
½ cup flour
1 stick margarine, softened
½ teaspoon nutmeg

1.  Preheat oven to 425°.

2.  Combine sugar, flour, cinnamon, and nutmeg. Sprinkle over sliced apples and toss. Place in pie shell.

3.  Mix topping ingredients and sprinkle over apples.

4.  Place pie in large, brown grocery bag; roll bag closed, secure with 2 paper clips.

5.  Remove top oven rack to keep bag from touching oven wall. Bake at 425° for 1 hour and 15 minutes.

**Serves 6-8.**

# TRAVIS' FAVORITE CARAMEL CRUNCH APPLE PIE

42 caramels
3 tablespoons water
3-4 cups tart cooking apples,
  peeled, cored, and sliced
1 9" unbaked pie shell
1 cup all-purpose flour
½ cup sugar
1 teaspoon cinnamon
½ cup butter or margarine
½ cup chopped walnuts or
  pecans (optional)

1.  Preheat oven to 375°.

2.  In double boiler, melt caramels with water. Layer apples and caramel sauce alternately in pie shell.

3.  Combine flour, sugar, and cinnamon. Cut in butter until consistency of coarse crumbs. Stir in nuts and sprinkle evenly over apples.

4.  Bake at 375° for 40-45 minutes. Serve hot with vanilla ice cream.

**Serves 6-8.**

# TURNER'S PINEAPPLE PIE

1 9" pie shell
**PIE FILLING**
1/4 cup flour
3/4 cup sugar
1/4 teaspoon salt
3/4 cup pineapple juice
1 cup boiling water
1 tablespoon butter
2 egg yolks (save whites for meringue)
1 (10¾-ounce) can crushed pineapple, drained
**MERINGUE**
2 egg whites
1/2 teaspoon vanilla extract
1/4 teaspoon cream of tartar
4 tablespoons sugar

1. Bake pie crust according to package directions.
2. Mix flour, sugar, and salt in 4-quart saucepan.
3. Add pineapple juice and boiling water. Bring to boil, stirring constantly until thick.
4. Remove from heat. Whip in egg yolks and butter. Stir in pineapple. Pour filling into baked pie shell and set aside.
5. Preheat broiler.
6. Beat egg whites with vanilla and cream of tartar until soft peaks form.
7. Gradually add sugar, beating until stiff and sugar dissolves.
8. Spread meringue on top of pie filling and place under broiler 3-5 minutes to brown. (Watch carefully.)

**Serves 6-8.**

# PECAN PIE

3 eggs
2/3 cup sugar
Dash of salt
2 tablespoons flour
1/2 teaspoon vanilla extract
1/3 cup butter, melted
1/2 cup light corn syrup
1/2 cup dark corn syrup
1 cup pecan halves
1 9" unbaked pie shell

1. Preheat oven to 350°.
2. Combine filling ingredients except pecans. Beat well, then add pecans.
3. Pour into unbaked pie shell and bake at 350° for 50 minutes.

**Serves 8.**

203

# GRANNY'S PECAN PIE

2 eggs
1 cup sugar
1 stick butter or margarine
1 tablespoon vinegar
1 tablespoon vanilla extract
¾ cup chopped pecans
½ cup raisins
½ cup coconut
1 8"-9" pie shell, unbaked

1. Preheat oven to 350°.
2. Beat eggs and sugar together. Add butter, vinegar, and vanilla.
3. Stir in pecans, raisins, and coconut.
4. Place in pie shell and bake at 350° for 50-55 minutes.

**Serves 8.**

# DAY AT THE RACES PIE

1 cup semi-sweet chocolate chips
½ cup walnuts, chopped
½ cup pecans, chopped
2 eggs, beaten
1 cup sugar
½ cup butter or margarine, melted
½ cup flour
1 teaspoon vanilla extract
1 9" unbaked pie shell
1 cup heavy cream, whipped

1. Preheat oven to 350°.
2. In large bowl, combine chocolate chips and nuts. Stir in next 5 ingredients and mix well by hand.
3. Pour into unbaked pie shell and bake at 350° for 30 minutes until toothpick comes out clean. Garnish with whipped cream.

**Serves 8-10.**

*Men love this!*

# No-Guilt Pumpkin Pie

⅔ cup sugar
½ teaspoon salt
1 teaspoon cinnamon
½ teaspoon ginger
¼ teaspoon cloves
Pinch of nutmeg
1 (16-ounce) can pumpkin
1 teaspoon vanilla extract
1 (12-ounce) can evaporated
   skim milk
½ teaspoon orange rind
   (careful to avoid the white
   pulp)
3 egg whites, slightly beaten
1 9" pie shell, unbaked

1. Preheat oven to 425°.
2. Combine first 6 ingredients.
3. Stir in pumpkin. Add vanilla, evaporated skim milk, orange rind, and egg whites. Beat with an electric mixer until smooth.
4. Pour into unbaked pie shell and bake 15 minutes at 425°.
5. Reduce heat to 350° and bake for 45 minutes until knife comes clean.

**Serves 8.**

*Pie filling has no fat, no cholesterol. With crust, each piece is about 200 calories.*

# Caribbean Fudge Pie

¼ cup butter, softened
¾ cup packed brown sugar
3 eggs
1 (12-ounce) package semi-
   sweet chocolate pieces,
   melted
2 teaspoons instant coffee
   powder
1 teaspoon rum extract
¼ cup flour
1 cup coarsely chopped
   walnuts
1 9" pie shell, unbaked
½ cup walnut halves for
   decoration
Whipped cream (optional)

1. Preheat oven to 375°.
2. Cream butter with sugar; beat in eggs, one at a time.
3. Add melted chocolate, instant coffee, and rum extract. Stir in flour and broken walnuts.
4. Pour mixture into pie shell and top with walnut halves. Bake at 375° for 25 minutes. Cool. Top with whipped cream, if desired.

**Serves 8.**

# CHOCOLATE PARADISE PIE

## MERINGUE CRUST

3 egg whites
1 cup sugar
½ cup chopped pecans
10 saltine crackers, loosely
   crumbled
¼ teaspoon salt

## FILLING

¾ cup milk
1 cup semi-sweet chocolate
   chips
3 egg yolks
Pinch of salt
1 tablespoon Kahlúa liqueur
   (optional)

## TOPPING

2 cups heavy cream
3 tablespoons sugar
3 (1.5-ounce) milk chocolate
   bars

1. Preheat oven to 300°.

2. For crust, beat egg whites until stiff. Gradually add remaining crust ingredients.

3. Bake crust in greased 9" x 2" pie plate at 300° for 35 minutes. Let cool.

4. For filling, heat milk to boiling. Place remaining filling ingredients in blender, add hot milk, and blend on low speed for 1 minute.

5. Pour into cooled pie shell and refrigerate 2-3 hours until set.

6. For topping, whip cream and add sugar. Pile on chilled filling and top with chocolate shavings or curls. (Try cheese slicer or vegetable peeler to make shavings.)

**Serves 8.**

*Friends will beg for this recipe.*

# Frozen Strawberry & Cream Pie

## Crust
1 cup flour
½ cup brown sugar
½ cup chopped nuts
½ cup butter, melted

## Strawberry Filling
1 cup heavy cream
2 egg whites
⅔ cup sugar
2 cups sliced strawberries
2 tablespoons lemon juice

1. Preheat oven to 350°.

2. Combine all ingredients for crust and spread evenly on cookie sheet. Bake at 350° for 20 minutes. Cool.

3. For filling, whip cream until stiff peaks form. Set aside.

4. Beat egg whites until stiff, gradually adding sugar. Gently fold egg whites into whipped cream. Add strawberries and lemon juice.

5. Crumble two-thirds crust mixture in bottom of 1-quart glass dish. Pour strawberry mixture over crust and top with remaining crust.

6. Freeze at least 6 hours. Before serving, refrigerate to thaw slightly.

**Serves 6-8.**

# PEACHES & CREAM CHEESE

## BATTER

¾ cup flour
1 teaspoon baking powder
½ teaspoon salt
1 (3¼-ounce) package French
vanilla pudding (not instant)
3 tablespoons butter or
margarine, softened
1 egg
½ cup milk

## FILLING

1 (15- to 20-ounce) can sliced
peaches, well drained with
juice reserved
1 (8-ounce) package cream
cheese, softened
½ cup sugar
3 tablespoons reserved juice

## TOPPING

3 tablespoons sugar
3 tablespoons cinnamon

1. Preheat oven to 350°.

2. Combine batter ingredients in
large mixing bowl. Beat 2
minutes at medium speed. Pour
into greased 9" x 9" x 2" pan or
9" x 2" pie plate.

3. Pour fruit over batter, reserving
juice.

4. Cream cheese, sugar, and
reserved juice. Beat 2 minutes at
medium speed. Spoon over fruit,
leaving ¾" edge.

5. Combine sugar and cinnamon.
Sprinkle over cream cheese
filling.

6. Bake at 350° for 30-35 minutes
until golden-brown crust. Serve
hot or cold.

**Serves 6-8.**

# PEACH COBBLER

2-3 cups fresh or canned
   peaches, drained and sliced
1 teaspoon cinnamon
1 tablespoon lemon juice
1 cup flour
1 teaspoon baking powder
½ teaspoon salt
3 tablespoons butter, softened
1¼ cups sugar, divided
½ cup milk
1 tablespoon cornstarch
1 cup boiling water

1. Preheat oven to 350°.
2. Line greased 13" x 9" x 2" pan with peaches. Sprinkle peaches with cinnamon and lemon juice.
3. Sift together flour, baking powder, and salt.
4. Cream butter, gradually adding ¾ cup sugar, and beat until fluffy.
5. Alternate one-third flour mixture and one-third milk to creamed butter and sugar until well mixed. Spread over peaches.
6. Combine remaining ½ cup sugar and cornstarch. Sprinkle over batter and slowly pour boiling water over entire mixture.
7. Bake at 350° for 1 hour. Serve with vanilla ice cream.

**Serves 6-8.**

# MOTHER'S APPLE COBBLER

½ cup brown sugar
½ cup flour
4 tablespoons butter, softened
4-5 pounds apples, peeled
   and sliced
1 teaspoon cinnamon
1 cup sugar
2 tablespoons flour
½ teaspoon salt
1 cup half-and-half

1. Preheat oven to 425°.
2. Cut butter into sugar and flour. Pat into 13" x 9" x 2" baking dish.
3. Sprinkle apples with cinnamon, then layer onto crust.
4. Combine sugar, flour, and salt. Add half-and-half and beat well.
5. Pour mixture over apples and bake at 425° for 1 hour.

**Serves 10.**

209

# APPLE CRISP

5-6 cups Granny Smith apples, peeled, cored, and thinly sliced
¾ cup quick-cooking rolled oats
¾ cup firmly packed brown sugar
½ cup flour
¼ teaspoon ground cinnamon
½ cup butter or margarine, softened
Heavy cream (optional)

1. Preheat oven to 350°.
2. Arrange apples in greased 8" x 1½" cake pan.
3. Combine oats, sugar, flour, and cinnamon. Cut butter into dry ingredients. Sprinkle mixture over apples.
4. Bake at 350° for 35-40 minutes. Serve warm with cream, if desired.

**Serves 6-8.**

# FRUIT PIZZA

¾-1 roll refrigerated sugar cookie dough
1 (8-ounce) package cream cheese, softened
⅓ cup sugar
1 (11-ounce) can mandarin oranges, drained
1-1½ bananas, sliced
1 medium bunch grapes, halved
½ pint strawberries, sliced
1 kiwi fruit, peeled and sliced

1. Preheat oven to 350°.
2. Pat cookie dough onto 12" pizza pan or baking stone leaving 1" edge.
3. Bake at 350° for 10-15 minutes until golden brown, then cool.
4. Combine cream cheese and sugar. Spread on cooled cookie crust.
5. Arrange orange sections around perimeter, pointing towards the center. Follow with banana slices, grape halves, and strawberry slices. Fill center of pizza with kiwi.
6. Sprinkle with sugar or drizzle with orange marmalade (heated in microwave for 30 seconds). Chill 1 hour before serving.

**Serves 12.**

# Apricot Parfait

1 (3-ounce) package lemon-flavored gelatin
1 (3-ounce) package orange-flavored gelatin
1 cup boiling water
3 cups apricot nectar
1 pint vanilla ice cream
Whipped cream and mint sprigs for garnish

1. Mix gelatin with boiling water until dissolved. Add apricot nectar. Add ice cream and stir until ice cream melts.

2. Let stand until mixture slightly thickens. Stir well and pour into parfait glasses or sherbet dishes.

3. Refrigerate until ready to serve, then garnish with whipped cream and sprig of mint.

**Yields 10 (½-cup) servings.**

# Winter Fruit with Lemon Yogurt Sauce

1 cup seedless red grapes, halved
1 cup seedless green grapes, halved
1 cup unpeeled, cubed, tart red apples
1 cup unpeeled, cubed, tart Granny Smith apples

**Lemon Yogurt Sauce**
8 ounces low-fat lemon yogurt
1 tablespoon honey
1 teaspoon grated lemon peel
½ teaspoon lemon extract
½ cup pecans, chopped

1. Combine fruits in medium-sized bowl.

2. In small bowl, mix sauce ingredients, except pecans.

3. Serve in individual dishes with sauce spooned over fruit. Sprinkle with pecans.

**Serves 8.**

*Delicious low-fat dessert.*

# CARUSO'S BOCCONE DOLCE

**MERINGUES**

4 egg whites
Dash of salt
¼ teaspoon cream of tartar
1 cup sugar

1 (6-ounce) package semi-
  sweet chocolate chips
3 tablespoons water
3 cups heavy cream
⅓ cup sugar
1 pint strawberries, sliced
  (save several whole ones for
  garnish)

1. Preheat oven to 250°.

2. Beat egg whites with salt and cream of tartar until stiff. Gradually add sugar. Beat until stiff and glossy.

3. Line three 8" cake pans (bottom and sides) with wax paper. Spread meringue on wax paper ¼"-½" thick.

4. Bake at 250° for 25-30 minutes until almost golden, but still pliable.

5. Peel paper from bottom and allow meringue to dry 2-3 hours on wire racks or overnight on paper.

6. Melt chocolate and water in double boiler.

7. Whip cream until almost stiff. Gradually add ⅓ cup sugar and beat until stiff.

8. Place 1 meringue on serving plate. Spread with thin layer of melted chocolate, ¾" layer of whipped cream, and layer of sliced strawberries. Repeat to top layer.

9. Decorate with whipped cream, whole berries, and drizzled chocolate.

**Serves 8-10.**

*Elegant dessert!*

# TIRAMISU

2½-3 cups cold espresso coffee (or instant espresso)
30 savoiardi (Italian ladyfingers)
8 egg yolks
8 tablespoons sugar
1 pound mascarpone cheese
1 tablespoon Marsala wine or rum
2 cups heavy cream
4 tablespoons cocoa powder

1. Pour cold coffee into large pie plate. Quickly dip half of ladyfingers in coffee. Line the bottom of 13" x 9" x 2" baking dish with dipped ladyfingers.

2. Whisk egg yolks and sugar until frothy, then add mascarpone and Marsala. Whisk until well blended and smooth.

3. In another bowl, whisk cream until stiff and fold into mascarpone mixture, blending well.

4. Pour half of mixture over ladyfingers. Dip remaining ladyfingers in coffee and arrange another layer over the mascarpone mixture.

5. Cover ladyfingers with remaining mascarpone, seal with plastic wrap, and chill at least 6 hours—best if overnight.

6. Sprinkle with sifted cocoa powder before serving.

**Serves 10.**

*If using regular ladyfingers, first toast at 350° for 15 minutes, then cool before dipping.*

# ENGLISH TRIFLE

## CUSTARD

¾ cup sugar
2 tablespoons cornstarch
⅛ teaspoon salt
2 cups half-and-half
4 egg yolks, beaten
2 tablespoons unsalted
   (sweet) butter
1½ teaspoons vanilla extract
1 cup heavy cream, whipped,
   plus ½ cup whipped cream
   for garnish

1 frozen pound cake
2 teaspoons sherry
Raspberry jam
Fresh or frozen peaches,
   strawberries, blueberries,
   and/or raspberries
Slivered almonds for garnish

1. For custard, combine sugar, cornstarch, and salt in double boiler. Water should be boiling but not touching top pan.

2. Stir in half-and-half, cover, and cook 8 minutes without stirring.

3. Uncover and cook 10 minutes, stirring constantly until sauce thickens and coats spoon.

4. Add beaten egg yolks and butter. Cook for 2 more minutes, then remove from heat. Stir occasionally to release heat or cool in refrigerator for 10 minutes.

5. Add vanilla and whipped cream. Set aside.

6. For shell, cut pound cake in half lengthwise and then into ½" slices.

7. Line large crystal bowl—bottom and sides—with cake, sprinkle with sherry, smooth on raspberry jam, fill curve with fruit (if frozen, drain well), and pour on custard.

8. Chill overnight and garnish with whipped cream and almonds.

**Serves 8-10.**

# LUSCIOUS LADYFINGER TRIFLE

8 ounces Baker's German
  sweet chocolate
3 tablespoons sugar
3 tablespoons cold water
4 egg yolks, well beaten
4 egg whites, well beaten and
  stiff
4 dozen ladyfinger cakes
Whipped cream

1. Melt chocolate in double boiler.
2. Add sugar, water, and egg yolks. Cook slowly, stirring constantly, until thick. Cool. Gently fold in egg whites.
3. Split ladyfingers and line sides and bottom of 2-quart trifle dish or straight-sided glass bowl.
4. Pour in layers of chocolate mixture alternating with layers of ladyfingers.
5. Chill for 24 hours and serve with fresh whipped cream.

**Serves 10.**

# CHERRY ROLL PUDDING

1 cup sugar
1 (16-ounce) can
  unsweetened cherries
**CAKE**
½ cup sugar
½ cup butter, softened
1 egg
1 cup flour
1 teaspoon vanilla extract

1. Preheat oven to 350°.
2. Bring sugar and cherries to boil. Pour into greased 8" or 10" square or round baking dish.
3. Mix together cake ingredients and drop by teaspoonfuls into cherry mixture.
4. Bake at 350° until cake is brown. Top with vanilla ice cream.

**Serves 8.**

# DATE-NUT PUDDING

3 eggs
1 cup sugar
3 tablespoons milk
1 teaspoon vanilla extract
3 tablespoons flour
2 teaspoons baking powder
½ teaspoon salt
2 cups coarsely chopped
dates
1 cup chopped pecans

**TOPPING**

1 cup heavy cream, chilled
3 tablespoons sugar
(granulated or powdered)

1. Preheat oven to 250°.

2. Beat eggs well. Beat in sugar until mixture thickens. Add milk and vanilla.

3. Combine flour, baking powder, and salt. Stir into egg mixture. Add dates and pecans.

4. Spread batter in greased 8½" x 4½" glass dish and bake at 250° for 40 minutes.

5. In chilled mixing bowl, beat cream and sugar until stiff.

6. Top pudding with whipped cream and serve warm or at room temperature.

**Serves 10.**

*A Christmas tradition.*

# PHIL'S FAVORITE CHOCOLATE MOUSSE

6 ounces semi-sweet
chocolate
2 tablespoons Kahlúa liqueur
1 tablespoon orange juice
2 egg yolks
2 whole eggs
¼ cup sugar
1 cup heavy cream
Whipped cream and
chocolate shavings for
garnish

1. Over low heat, melt chocolate with Kahlúa and orange juice. Set aside.

2. In blender, mix egg yolks and eggs with sugar for 2 minutes. Add whipping cream. Blend 30 seconds. Add chocolate mixture and blend until smooth.

3. Serve in champagne or parfait glasses. Garnish with whipped cream and chocolate shavings.

**Serves 4.**

# BOULEY-INSPIRED HOT CHOCOLATE SOUFFLÉ

6 3"-4" ramekins

Butter and sugar for ramekin lining

2 ounces and 6 ¼-ounce chunks semi-sweet or bittersweet chocolate

4 tablespoons unsalted (sweet) butter

¼ cup heavy cream

⅓ cup cocoa powder

3 egg yolks

4 egg whites

2 tablespoons sugar

1. Preheat oven to 400°.

2. Butter ramekins and coat sides with sugar.

3. Melt 2 ounces chocolate and butter in double boiler.

4. Warm cream over low heat.

5. Add warm cream, cocoa powder, and egg yolks to chocolate mixture. Mix well.

6. Beat egg whites to soft peaks. Add sugar and beat slowly to create a meringue.

7. Remove chocolate mixture from heat. Fold one-fourth the meringue into chocolate, then fold chocolate into remaining meringue.

8. Pour mixture into ramekins. Drop 1 chunk of chocolate into each ramekin.

9. Bake at 400° for 8 minutes on cookie sheet.

**Serves 6.**

*Easiest to prepare steps 1-5 before dinner.*

*Very impressive dessert.*

# PRALINE SUNDAE SAUCE

⅓ cup water
⅓ cup brown sugar, packed
1 cup light corn syrup
1 cup chopped pecans
⅛ teaspoon rum extract
⅛ teaspoon maple or vanilla extract

1. Combine water, sugar, and corn syrup in saucepan. Cook slowly until mixture comes to boil.
2. Add nuts and extracts. Cool, cover, and refrigerate.
3. To serve, spoon sauce over ice cream.

**Yields 1 pint.**

# MARY MUMPHREY'S CREAMY PRALINES

1 cup light brown sugar, packed
1 cup granulated sugar
⅔ cup evaporated milk
1½ tablespoons vanilla extract
1½-2 cups pecan halves
1½ tablespoons butter
Candy thermometer

1. In a 3-quart saucepan, combine first 3 ingredients. Cook slowly to 248°.
2. Add remaining ingredients, beating mixture until it starts to shine and thicken.
3. Drop by spoonfuls on wax paper and let cool.

**Yields 3-3½ dozen.**

*To prevent wax paper from sticking to counter, cover counter with newspaper first.*

*For chocolate pralines, add cocoa powder.*

# Mom's Divinity Candy

2 egg whites
4 cups sugar
1 cup light corn syrup
1 cup boiling water
2 cups chopped pecans or
  walnuts
1 teaspoon vanilla extract

1. Beat egg whites to stiff peaks.
2. Combine sugar, corn syrup, and water in saucepan. Bring to boil and continue cooking, without stirring, to the soft-ball stage.
3. At the soft-ball stage, slowly pour syrup over egg whites. Beat until mixture thickens and begins to lose its gloss.
4. Quickly stir in vanilla and nuts, then quickly drop by teaspoonfuls onto wax paper.
5. Allow to dry completely before storing tightly covered.

**Yields 3-4 dozen.**

# Caramel Popcorn

5 quarts popcorn, popped
1 cup butter, melted
2 cups brown sugar
½ cup dark corn syrup
1 teaspoon salt
½ teaspoon baking soda
2 cups peanuts

1. Preheat oven to 250°.
2. In 2-quart saucepan, mix butter, brown sugar, corn syrup, and salt. Boil gently for 5 minutes. Stir in baking soda and peanuts.
3. Pour over popcorn and mix well.
4. Spread popcorn out on two greased 13" x 9" x 2" baking dishes (non-stick if available) and bake at 250° for 1 hour, stirring every 15 minutes. When done, remove immediately from pan to prevent sticking.

**Serves 10-12.**

# CAJUN CHRISTMAS LOG

1 (1-pound) box graham crackers
1 (10-ounce) jar cherries, sliced
1 (9-ounce) box raisins
2 cups chopped pecans
1 (7-ounce) bag coconut
1 (14-ounce) can condensed milk

1. Crush graham crackers. Mix two-thirds with remaining ingredients.
2. Sprinkle remaining crumbs on square sheet of foil. Roll half the cherry mixture in crumbs to form a log. Roll log in foil and close ends.
3. Repeat, making second log with remaining cherry mixture.
4. Freeze logs. When ready to serve, remove from freezer for about 30 minutes and slice in ¼" slices.

**Serves 10-12.**

# HOLIDAY STOVE-TOP POTPOURRI

4 oranges, cut into eighths
2 lemons, cut into eighths
6 cinnamon sticks, broken in half
4 teaspoons whole cloves
2 teaspoons whole allspice
8 bay leaves

1. Combine all ingredients and place in airtight container or divide into 4 gift jars.
2. When ready to fill home with wonderful aroma, combine potpourri with water in saucepan and simmer.

*Can be re-used—just refrigerate and, when ready to use, add more water and simmer.*

# KIDS' CREATIONS

KIDS' CREATIONS

## Good Starts

## Great Adventures

## Sweet Dreams

# "MY KID WILL EAT IT" OATMEAL

¼ cup quick-cooking oats
¼ cup apple juice, white
  grape, pear, or other
  favorite juice
¼ cup water
2-3 tablespoons applesauce,
  mashed banana, pears,
  peaches, or yogurt

1. Combine oats, juice, and water in 16-18 ounce microwaveable bowl. Microwave on high 1½-2 minutes.

2. Stir in fruit or yogurt and serve.

**Serves 1.**

*Can be halved for less hearty appetites.*

# GREEN EGGS & HAM

The book by Dr. Seuss
3 eggs
1-2 tablespoons milk
3 drops green food coloring
2 slices ham

1. Read the book.

2. Beat eggs with milk and food coloring.

3. Scramble eggs and serve with ham.

**Serves 2.**

# FROZEN BANANA TREATS

1 bunch bananas
Juice of 1 lemon

1. Peel bananas and place side by side in baking dish.

2. Squeeze lemon juice over bananas and freeze.

**Serves 6-8.**

# BANANA BITTIES

1 banana
Peanut butter
Wheat germ (plain or honey)

1. Slice banana into ¼" rounds
2. Spread each slice with peanut butter, then sprinkle with wheat germ.
3. Serve immediately or chill 5 minutes in refrigerator.

**Serves 1-2.**

*Can substitute apple slices for banana.*

# BANANA SMOOTHIE

1 large banana
1½ cups milk
½ teaspoon vanilla extract
1 tablespoon honey (optional)

1. Blend all ingredients.
2. Serve at once.

**Serves 1-2.**

*May use any favorite fruit. Great for toddlers who won't drink their milk.*

# WEE COOKS' APPLE BUTTER

6 unpeeled, uncored apples, quartered
½ cup water
⅓ cup sugar
½ teaspoon lemon juice
Cinnamon to taste
4 tablespoons butter

1. Place quartered apples, water, sugar, and lemon juice in saucepan. Bring to boil, then simmer until apples are tender.
2. Press ingredients through sieve, removing apple skin and seeds.
3. Add cinnamon to taste, whip in butter, and enjoy with favorite bread or waffles.

**Yields 2 cups.**

# GRANNY'S WHITE BREAD

1 (12-ounce) can evaporated milk
2 cans water
2 (¼-ounce) packages dry yeast
1 cup sugar
1 teaspoon salt
2 tablespoons vegetable shortening
7 cups flour

1. Preheat oven to 380°.

2. In a large bowl, combine all ingredients except flour. Add enough flour to make dough easy to handle.

3. Cover with towel and let rise about 1 hour until dough doubles in height.

4. Butter four 8" x 4" x 2½" loaf pans.

5. Divide dough into 4 sections. Turn one quarter onto lightly floured board. Knead, adding flour as needed for firm, dry consistency. Press into buttered pan.

6. Repeat steps with remaining quarters. Cover pans with towels and let rise for 1 hour until doubled in height again.

7. Bake at 380° for 45 minutes.

**Yields 4 loaves.**

*Kids love this toasted with butter or peanut butter and jelly.*

# "PINK STUFF"

1 (15-ounce) can crushed pineapple, drained
1 (20-ounce) can cherry pie filling
1 (14-ounce) can sweetened condensed milk
5½ ounces mini-marshmallows
1 cup chopped pecans (optional)
1 (8-ounce) tub Cool Whip
1 (3½-ounce) can coconut flakes

1. Combine all ingredients to-gether.
2. Refrigerate overnight before serving.

**Serves 12.**

# PRETZEL SALAD

2¼ cup pretzels, broken into small pieces
1 stick melted margarine
3 tablespoons and 1 cup sugar
1 (8-ounce) package cream cheese
1 (8-ounce) tub Cool Whip
2 (3-ounce) packages strawberry-flavored gelatin
2 cups boiling water
2 packages frozen strawberries, thawed

1. Preheat oven to 350°.
2. Combine pretzels, margarine, and 3 tablespoons sugar. Press into 13" x 9" x 2" baking dish to make crust. Bake at 350° for 10 minutes, then cool.
3. Blend remaining cup of sugar and cream cheese. Fold in Cool Whip. Spread over pretzel mixture.
4. Dissolve gelatin in boiling water and add thawed fruit. Pour over top and refrigerate until set.

**Serves 12.**

*Recipe can be halved.*

# HOLIDAY BUNNIES

6 lettuce leaves
6 pear halves
12 slivered almonds (2 per bunny)
12 cloves (2 per bunny)
6 miniature marshmallows
2 slices American cheese
6 parsley sprigs

1. To make each bunny, place 1 lettuce leaf on individual salad plate as "grass" and place 1 pear half on each lettuce leaf as bunny.

2. Place 2 almonds for "ears" on small end of pear; place 2 cloves for "eyes" in front of almonds; and place marshmallow for "tail" at large end of pear half.

3. Mold small piece of American cheese to carrot shape. Insert small sprig of parsley in end of "carrot" and place at bunny's "mouth."

**Yields 6 bunnies.**

*May substitute real carrot slice for cheese.*

# RED DEVIL

1 (10¾-ounce) can tomato soup, undiluted
¾ cup grated Cheddar or American cheese
Dash of Worcestershire sauce
8 slices toasted, buttered bread

1. Heat tomato soup and add cheese, stirring to melt. Add dash of Worcestershire sauce.

2. Pour hot mixture over two slices toast and garnish with carrot and celery sticks.

**Serves 4.**

# PORCUPINE SALAD

3 pear halves
3 lettuce leaves
15-20 almonds, slivered
6 raisins

1. Place pear halves face down on lettuce leaves.
2. For porcupine "quills," stick almond slivers in large end of pear.
3. Decorate with raisin "eyes" on thin end of pear.

**Yields 3 porcupines.**

*Serve with Porcupine Meatballs.*

# PORCUPINE MEATBALLS

1 pound ground beef, turkey, or chicken
½ cup rice, cooked
3 green onions, chopped
½ bell pepper, chopped
1 tablespoon Worcestershire sauce
1 (10¾-ounce) can tomato soup, undiluted
½ cup water

1. Preheat oven to 350°.
2. Combine first 5 ingredients. Add 1 tablespoon undiluted tomato soup. Roll into 6-8 balls and place in 1-quart casserole dish.
3. Mix remaining soup with water. Pour over meatballs, cover tightly with foil, and bake at 350° for 30 minutes.

**Serves 4.**

*Serve with Porcupine Salad.*

# MOMMY'S STEALTH MEAT LOAF

Chopped carrots, broccoli, beans, peas, and any other vegetables of choice
2 pounds lean ground beef
2 cups fresh bread crumbs (about 4 bread slices)
½ cup milk
½ cup minced onions
2 eggs
2 teaspoons salt
¼ teaspoon pepper
1 teaspoon minced garlic (optional)

1. Steam vegetables, then puree in blender or food processor.
2. Preheat oven to 350°.
3. In large bowl, combine pureed vegetables with remaining ingredients, mixing well. Spoon mixture into 9" x 5" loaf and level top.
4. Bake at 350° for 1½ hours. Let stand 5 minutes at room temperature, then pour off meat drippings. Loosen loaf with spatula and invert onto warm platter.

**Serves 8.**

# EASY BEEF ENCHILADAS

1 pound ground beef
1 medium onion, chopped
1 (10-ounce) can mushroom soup
1 (10½-ounce) can enchilada sauce
⅓ cup milk
1 (4-ounce) can chopped green chilies
8-10 fajita-sized flour tortillas
2½ cups grated Cheddar and/or Monterey Jack cheese
½ cup chopped pitted ripe olives (optional)

1. Preheat oven to 400°.
2. In a 10" skillet, brown meat and onions. Drain grease.
3. Stir in mushroom soup, enchilada sauce, milk, and chilies. Reduce heat, cover, and cook 20 minutes, stirring occasionally.
4. Soften tortillas in microwave according to package. Place equal amounts of cheese and sprinkle of olives on each tortilla. Roll up and place in lightly greased 13" x 9" x 2" baking dish.
5. Cover with sauce and cook at 400° for 40 minutes.

**Serves 6-8.**

# AUNT FRAN'S TATER TOT CASSEROLE

2 pounds ground chuck
1 (26-ounce) jar spaghetti
   sauce, less if desired
1 (11-ounce) can Cheddar
   cheese soup
Portion of 1 (28-ounce) bag
   frozen potato puffs

1. Preheat oven to 350°.
2. Brown ground chuck, drain, add spaghetti sauce, and mix well.
3. Transfer to 8" round casserole dish. (Beef should make a 2" layer.)
4. Spread Cheddar cheese soup across beef.
5. Stick potato puffs into soup, round side up. Work from outside of circle and move inward. (Kids love this part!)
6. Bake at 350° for 20-30 minutes until bubbling.

**Serves 4-6.**

# HAMBURGER, MACARONI, & CHEESE

1 (7¼-ounce) box macaroni
   and cheese
1 pound ground beef
1 (10¾-ounce) can cream of
   mushroom soup
½ cup milk

1. Preheat oven to 350°.
2. Cook macaroni and cheese as directed.
3. Brown and season ground beef. Drain fat and add remaining ingredients.
4. In 11" x 7" x 2" baking dish, layer macaroni and cheese with ground beef mixture, beginning with macaroni and ending with ground beef.
5. Bake at 350° for 30-45 minutes until bubbly.

**Serves 4-6.**

# FAMILY TREE TORTELLINI

2 packages frozen tortellini with meat
1 (32-ounce) jar spaghetti sauce
8 ounces mozzarella cheese, shredded

1. Preheat oven to 350°.
2. Boil tortellini in 4-6 quarts water for 8-9 minutes. Drain.
3. Grease 13" x 9" x 2" pan. Spread with one-third spaghetti sauce, cover with tortellini, add remaining sauce, and top with cheese.
4. Bake at 350° for 30 minutes until bubbly.

**Serves 6-8.**

# CHICKEN NUGGETS

1 pound boneless, skinless chicken breasts, cut in 1" cubes
2 tablespoons margarine, melted
2 tablespoons milk
4 slices whole wheat bread
1/4 cup grated Parmesan cheese
3 garlic cloves, minced (or 1/2 teaspoon garlic powder)
1/2 teaspoon salt

1. Preheat oven to 375° and line cookie sheet with foil.
2. Combine margarine and milk in bowl. Add chicken cubes to coat well. Drain.
3. Grind bread in food processor or blender to make crumbs.
4. Combine bread crumbs, cheese, garlic, and salt in plastic or paper bag. Add chicken and shake to coat chicken.
5. Bake at 375° for 12-15 minutes until done, turning halfway through.

**Serves 4-6.**

*Freeze leftovers and defrost a few at a time for a quick meal.*

# REPORT CARD DAY COOKIES

2 cups brown sugar
2 cups granulated sugar
3/4 cup butter, softened
1 cup vegetable shortening
4 eggs
2 teaspoons vanilla extract
3 cups flour
2 teaspoons salt
2 teaspoons baking soda
3 cups uncooked rolled oats
2 cups coconut
2 cups raisins
1 cup chocolate chips
1 cup chopped nuts

1. Preheat oven to 350°.

2. Cream together sugars, butter, and shortening. Beat in eggs and vanilla.

3. Combine flour, salt, and soda, then beat into first mixture.

4. Gradually add remaining ingredients.

5. Drop by heaping teaspoonfuls spaced 2″ apart on greased cookie sheet.

6. Bake at 350° for 8 minutes until browned.

**Yields 7 dozen**

*May shape dough into rolls, wrap, and chill several hours or freeze. Then slice and bake as directed.*

# BIG MAC COOKIES

1 can vanilla icing
(The Mustard)
1 small package coconut (The Lettuce)
Yellow and green food coloring
1 box vanilla wafers (The Bun)
2 packages Haviland chocolate mints (The Meat)
1 egg white
Sesame seeds

1. Tint icing yellow and coconut green with food coloring.

2. Spread small amount of icing on flat side of vanilla wafer, then layer mint, more icing, a sprinkle of coconut, and another wafer on top.

3. Let "burger" stand 15 minutes to harden icing, then put a drop of egg white on top wafer and press on sesame seeds.

**Yields as many as you can eat!**

*Since these are "no-bake" cookies, children can do all the work.*

# MONSTER COOKIES

½ cup margarine, softened
1 cup sugar
1 cup plus 2 tablespoons brown sugar
3 eggs
2 cups peanut butter
¾ tablespoon light corn syrup
¼ teaspoon vanilla extract
4½ cups regular oats
2 teaspoons baking soda
¼ teaspoon salt
1½ cups M&M's

1. Preheat oven to 350°.

2. Cream margarine and sugars. Add eggs, peanut butter, corn syrup, and vanilla. Beat well.

3. Add oats, baking soda, and salt. Stir in M&M's. Mixture will be thick.

4. Drop by heaping teaspoonfuls onto ungreased cookie sheet and bake at 350° for 10-12 minutes

**Yields 6 dozen.**

*A lunch box dessert favorite!*

# HONEY PEANUT COOKIES

⅓ cup honey
½ cup peanut butter
¼ teaspoon cinnamon
1 cup instant non-fat milk
    powder
½ cup crushed corn flakes

1.  Combine all ingredients except
    corn flakes in medium-sized
    bowl. Stir in corn flakes.

2.  Shape into 6″ roll on wax paper.
    Wrap tightly and chill. Cut into
    ¼″ slices and serve.

**Yields 24 slices.**

# FLOWER POT DESSERT

1 (1¼-pound) package Oreos
1 (8-ounce) package cream
    cheese
½ stick margarine, room
    temperature
½ (14-ounce) can sweetened
    condensed milk
2 (3⅝-ounce) packages
    instant French vanilla
    pudding
2¼ cups milk
1 (12-ounce) tub Cool Whip
8″ plastic flower pot
Plastic wrap
Gummy worms
Real or artificial flowers, stem
    wrapped in plastic wrap
Garden shovel

1.  Crush Oreos in food processor
    and divide into 3 parts.

2.  Cream together cream cheese,
    margarine, and condensed milk.
    Blend in pudding and milk, then
    fold in Cool Whip.

3.  Cover bottom of flower pot with
    plastic wrap. Layer with one-
    third cookie crumbs, then half
    the cream cheese mixture, one-
    third cookie crumbs, and re-
    maining cream cheese mixture.
    Top with remaining cookie
    crumbs.

4.  Decorate with gummy worms
    and flowers. Use clean garden
    shovel to serve.

**Serves 8-10.**

# OREO COOKIE DESSERT

1 (1¼-pound) package Oreos
½-¾ cup margarine
½ gallon vanilla ice cream
1 (8-ounce) can chocolate
  syrup
1 (8-ounce) tub Cool Whip
Pecans (optional)

1. Crumble Oreo cookies by hand to cover bottom of any size casserole dish. Melt margarine and pour over crust, patting down slightly.
2. Cut ¾" thick slices ice cream. Place over crust. Pour chocolate syrup over ice cream.
3. Freeze for 30 minutes. Remove from freezer and cover with Cool Whip and pecans.
4. Freeze another 2 hours before serving. Cover after cutting.

**Serves 8-10.**

*Stays fresh in freezer up to 1 week.*

# OREO COOKIE ICE CREAM CAKE

2 (1¼-pound) packages Oreos
¾ stick butter, melted
1 gallon vanilla ice cream, softened

1. Scoop out middle of Oreos and discard or eat. Blend cookies in food processor to crumbs.
2. Combine melted butter with 2½ cups crumbs and spread on bottom and sides of 10" springform pan.
3. Mix ice cream with remaining crumbs until consistency of custard, then pour over cookie crust. Cover with foil and freeze.

**Serves 10-12.**

# LADYFINGER PUDDING CAKE

1 package (about 8)
ladyfingers
1 (4-ounce) package vanilla
pudding (not instant)
1 (4-ounce) package
chocolate pudding (not
instant)

1. Line bottom of 8" x 8" x 2" glass dish with ladyfingers.

2. Cook vanilla pudding according to package directions and pour over ladyfingers.

3. Refrigerate until pudding sets.

4. Add another layer of ladyfingers on top.

5. Cook chocolate pudding according to package directions and pour over second layer of ladyfingers. (Cake will float to top)

6. Refrigerate until pudding sets. Cover with plastic wrap to keep soft.

**Serves 8.**

*May use leftover cake instead of ladyfingers.*

# QUICKIE CHEESECAKES

18 foil cupcake liners
18 vanilla wafers
2 eggs
½ cup sugar
2 (8-ounce) packages cream
cheese, softened
2 teaspoons vanilla extract
1 (21-ounce) can cherry or
blueberry pie filling

1. Preheat oven to 375°.

2. Place liners on cookie sheet. Place one vanilla wafer in each.

3. Blend eggs, sugar, cream cheese, and vanilla in blender until smooth.

4. Fill liners with mixture, about ¾ full. Bake at 375° for 12-15 minutes. Let cool.

5. Spoon pie filling on top of each and chill before serving.

**Yields 18 mini cheesecakes.**

# LEMON CHEESECAKE

## CRUST
1¼ cups graham cracker
  crumbs
3 tablespoons sugar
⅓ cup melted butter
¼ cup chopped pecans

## FILLING
1 (3-ounce) package lemon-
  flavored gelatin
1¼ cups boiling water
1 (8-ounce) package cream
  cheese, softened
1 cup sugar
5 tablespoons lemon juice
1 (12-ounce) can evaporated
  milk, chilled
Graham cracker crumbs for
  topping

1. Mix crust ingredients and press into 13" x 9" x 2" pan.
2. Dissolve gelatin in boiling water. Cool. Mix cream cheese, sugar, and lemon juice. Add to cooled gelatin.
3. Whip evaporated milk and fold into gelatin mixture. Pour into crust and sprinkle with graham cracker crumbs. Chill overnight.

**Serves 8.**

# LEMON PIE

1 (8-ounce) tub Cool Whip
¾ cup lemon juice
1 (14-ounce) can sweetened
  condensed milk
1 9" graham cracker crust

1. Combine first 3 ingredients.
2. Pour into graham cracker crust and chill.

**Serves 8.**

*Can add small can of drained, crushed pineapple to the filling.*

# BLUEBERRY-BANANA PIE

2 9" pie shells
3-4 bananas
1 (8-ounce) package cream cheese, softened
1 cup sugar
1 cup heavy cream
1 (21-ounce) can blueberry pie filling

1. Bake pie shells according to package directions. Cool, then slice bananas in bottom of pie crusts.

2. Combine cream cheese and sugar. Beat whipping cream until thick, then add to cream cheese mixture. Pour over bananas.

3. Top pie with blueberry filling and refrigerate.

**Yields 2 pies.**

# QUICKIE FRUIT COBBLER

1 cup flour
⅔ cup sugar
2½ teaspoons baking powder
¼ teaspoon salt (optional)
1 cup whole or skim milk
4 tablespoons butter or margarine, melted
4 cups fruit (canned or fresh peaches, blueberries, apples, etc.)
1 teaspoon cinnamon

1. Preheat oven to 350°.

2. In bowl, combine flour, sugar, baking powder, and salt. Stir in milk and mix batter until smooth.

3. Pour melted butter or margarine into 8" x 8" x 2" baking dish. Pour in batter and cover all with fruit. Sprinkle with cinnamon and sugar.

4. Bake at 350° for 40 to 45 minutes until lightly browned.

**Serves 6-8.**

*Quick, easy, and adored by all!*

# Aunt Mary's Faux Éclairs

2 (3-ounce) packages instant vanilla pudding
3 cups milk
1 (8-ounce) tub Cool Whip
Club or Waverly crackers
1 (1-pound) can dark chocolate frosting (microwave for easy spreading)

1. Mix vanilla pudding with milk until well blended. Mix in Cool Whip.
2. In 13" x 9" x 2" baking dish, layer crackers and pudding mixture twice, then top with more crackers.
3. Spread chocolate frosting on top.
4. Cover and refrigerate overnight.

**Serves 12-15.**

# Tiger Butter

12 ounces white chocolate
1 heaping tablespoon smooth peanut butter
6 ounces semi-sweet chocolate chips, less if desired

1. Line cookie sheet with wax paper.
2. Melt white chocolate on low in microwave, stirring often.
3. Stir in peanut butter and spread onto lined cookie sheet.
4. Melt chocolate chips in microwave, then swirl into white chocolate mixture.
5. Freeze for quick setting, then break into pieces.

**Yields about 2 dozen.**

# APRIL'S PEANUT BUTTER BALLS

1 cup smooth peanut butter
1 cup sugar
1 cup Rice Crispies
½ cup powdered chocolate-
   milk mix
Raisins (optional)

1. Cream together peanut butter and sugar in mixing bowl. Add Rice Crispies, mix well.

2. Scoop up teaspoonfuls of mixture and roll into 1" balls. Place raisin "surprise" in center of each.

3. Roll each ball in chocolate powder, coating thoroughly. Refrigerate until ready to serve.

**Yields 3 dozen.**

# CHOCOLATE PEANUT CLUSTERS

1 (12-ounce) package semi-
   sweet chocolate chips
1 (6-ounce) package peanut
   butter chips
1 cup Spanish peanuts

1. Melt chocolate and peanut butter chips together in microwave. Stir in peanuts.

2. Drop by teaspoonfuls onto wax paper. Freeze for quick setting.

**Serves 8.**

# Index

242

## FAMILY CREATIONS
Madison Square Station
P.O. Box 1152
New York, N.Y. 10159

Send me _____ copies of FAMILY CREATIONS @ $15.95  each   _____
Add postage & handling @   $3.00  each   _____
**TOTAL ENCLOSED**   _____

Name _____

Address_____

City _____ State _____ Zip_____

Phone _____

Make check payable to THE GLADNEY FUND or
Charge to  ☐ Mastercard   ☐ Visa
☐☐☐☐-☐☐☐☐-☐☐☐☐-☐☐☐☐

Expiration Date: _____

Signature: _____

- - - - - - - - - - - - - - - - - - - - - - - - - - - - -

## FAMILY CREATIONS
Madison Square Station
P.O. Box 1152
New York, N.Y. 10159

Send me _____ copies of FAMILY CREATIONS @ $15.95  each   _____
Add postage & handling @   $3.00  each   _____
**TOTAL ENCLOSED**   _____

Name _____

Address_____

City _____ State _____ Zip_____

Phone _____

Make check payable to THE GLADNEY FUND or
Charge to  ☐ Mastercard   ☐ Visa
☐☐☐☐-☐☐☐☐-☐☐☐☐-☐☐☐☐

Expiration Date: _____

Signature: _____